one-pan
KITCHEN

120 delicious homemade meals made in your skillet

Copyright © 2016 StoreBound, LLC.

All rights reserved.

No part of this book may be reproduced or transmitted in any manner whatsoever without written permission from StoreBound, except in the case of brief quotation embodied in editorial articles or reviews.

Dash
50 Broad Street, New York, NY 10004

ISBN 978-0-9971012-0-1

Printed in India
10 9 8 7 6 5 4 3 2 1
First Edition

Distributed by StoreBound
50 Broad Street, New York, NY 10004

Executive Director: Evan Dash
Editorial Director: Catherine-Gail Reinhard
Executive Food Editor: Caitlin Wise
Editor: Gina Picardo
Art Director: Florence Ko
Staff Photographer: Julian Master

Recipe Contributors (A-Z):
Sunny Choi
Evan Dash
Slim Geransar
Rachel Hecht
Melissa Holmes
Florence Ko
Jennifer Lonergan
Shaun MacKenzie
Julian Master
Gina Picardo
Giselle Regino
Catherine-Gail Reinhard
Elizabeth Skinner
Caitlin Wise

Contents

4 - 5	Introduction
6 – 33	30 Minute Meals
34 – 51	Breakfast
52 – 69	Eggs
70 – 99	Appetizers
100 – 127	Soups & Stews
128 – 193	Entrées
194 – 229	Sides
230 – 257	Desserts

Introduction

How many pans does it take to make dinner? We think that if the answer to that question is two, that's one too many. Too often, recipe books call for using so many pots and pans that you need a full-time dishwasher to clean up after you're done cooking.

One-Pan Kitchen is our answer to that problem. With 120 recipes that you can make using your Dash Skillet, this book shows you how to braise, boil, sear, stir-fry and sauté your way to satisfying and delicious home-cooked meals in a dash.

To develop our recipes, we've used the Dash 14" Family Size Rapid Skillet, but the recipes can also be adapted to work on the stovetop with a large French skillet or sauté pan.

We've all contributed some of our best go-to recipes to this book and we hope that some of these become family favorites that you make over and over again.

At Dash, we believe that the path to health and wellness starts with cooking at home. From our headquarters in New York City, our team works tirelessly to develop tools that make it easier for you to prepare and enjoy home-cooked meals using natural, unprocessed ingredients.

Our mission is to make it easier to prepare real food at home so that you can feel your best.

That's what living unprocessed is all about.

Chicken Schnitzel pg 26-27

30 Minute Meals

8-9   Macaroni & Cheese

10-11   Swiss Baked Macaroni & Cheese with Mushrooms

12-13   Vegetable Stir-Fry

14-15   Moroccan Couscous

16-17   Skillet Pizza

18-19   Skillet Baked Ziti

20-21   Spicy Sausage Penne

22-23   Baked Tortellini

24-25   Chicken & Orzo Skillet Casserole

26-27   Chicken Schnitzel

28-29   Beef Quesadilla

30-31   Beef Fajitas

32-33   Meatballs & Mozzarella Bake

Macaroni & Cheese

Servings: 6–8   **Time:** 25 minutes

Ingredients

1 lb macaroni

1½ cups half & half or whole milk

1 egg

1 tsp mustard

1 tbsp ketchup

½ tsp onion powder

8 oz cheddar cheese, grated

8 oz Muenster cheese, grated

¼ cup (½ stick) butter

Directions

Place macaroni in the skillet and cover with water. Add a teaspoon of salt to the water. Turn the skillet on high and bring the water to a boil, stirring occasionally.

Once water is boiling, lower the temperature to medium to bring the water to a low boil. Cook pasta for about 8 more minutes or until al dente, stirring occasionally.

While pasta is boiling, whisk together the half & half, egg, mustard, ketchup, and onion powder in a medium bowl. Drain the pasta and then place back in the skillet over medium low heat. Add the butter and the milk mixture to the skillet and stir.

Once the butter has melted, add the two cheeses. Stir until everything is melted and creamy. Season with salt and pepper, if desired.

Swiss Macaroni & Cheese with Mushrooms

Servings: 6-8   **Time:** 30 minutes

Ingredients

1 lb macaroni

1½ cups half & half or whole milk

1 egg

1 tsp mustard

1 tbsp ketchup

½ tsp onion powder

8 oz Swiss cheese, grated

8 oz Muenster cheese, grated

¼ cup (½ stick) butter

8 oz button mushrooms

1 cup cooked ham, diced (optional)

1 cup fresh or frozen green peas

Directions

Slice mushrooms and sauté in the skillet in 1 tablespoon of butter. Set aside.

Place macaroni in the skillet and cover with water. Add a teaspoon of salt to the water.

Turn the skillet on high and bring the water to a boil, stirring occasionally. Once water is boiling, lower the temperature to medium to bring the water to a low boil. Cook pasta for about 8 more minutes or until al dente, stirring occasionally.

While pasta is boiling, whisk together the half & half, egg, mustard, ketchup, and onion powder in a medium bowl. Drain the pasta and then place it back in the skillet over medium low heat. Stir in the remaining butter and milk mixture.

Once the butter has melted, add the two cheeses. Stir until everything is melted and creamy.

Add in the sautéed mushrooms, ham, and green peas. Season with salt and pepper, if desired.

Vegetable Stir-Fry

Servings: 8-10   **Time:** 30 minutes

Ingredients

1 red bell pepper, thinly sliced
1 yellow bell pepper, thinly sliced
1 crown broccoli, cut into florets
3 large carrots, thinly sliced
2 cups snow peas
2 cups green onions, chopped
3 cloves garlic, minced
1 tsp sesame oil
1 tbsp soy sauce
1 tbsp sesame seeds
salt and pepper, to taste

Directions

Set your skillet to medium low heat. Add the peppers, broccoli, carrots, snow peas, and green onions to the skillet.

While stirring the vegetables, add in the garlic, sesame oil, soy sauce, salt, and pepper.

Cover with the lid, and cook for about 10-15 minutes, stirring occasionally. The vegetables should be crunchy but not hard.

Top with sesame seeds. Serve over a scoop of white or brown rice.

Moroccan Couscous

Servings: 6-8   **Time:** 30 minutes

Ingredients

4 cups couscous
6 cups organic chicken broth
1 medium red onion, diced
1 yellow or red bell pepper, cut into 1" pieces
1 green bell pepper, cut into 1" pieces
3 plum tomatoes, quartered
2 cups chickpeas
½ cup golden raisins
½ cup sliced almonds
1 tbsp grated orange zest
4 tbsp olive oil, divided
1 cup pomegranate arils (seeds), to garnish
salt and pepper, to taste

Moroccan spice mixture:
1 tsp allspice
1 tsp cardamom
1 tsp coriander
1 tsp cumin
1 tsp cinnamon

Directions

Sauté the onion, bell peppers, and tomatoes in 3 tablespoons olive oil over medium heat for 4 minutes or until the vegetables soften. Add the chickpeas to the pan and cook an additional 3 minutes, stirring frequently. Add the almonds and golden raisins and toast for 30 seconds. Remove from pan and set aside. In a bowl, sift together all ingredients for the spice mixture.

Heat skillet over medium. Add 1 tablespoon olive oil to the pan with orange zest and 1 tablespoon of the Moroccan spice mixture. When the spices become fragrant, add the chicken broth. Increase heat to high and bring the broth to a boil.

Turn off the heat, add the couscous to the broth and mix thoroughly. Cover with the lid for 10 minutes.

Add the vegetables to the couscous and mix. Cover and let sit for an additional 3 minutes. Uncover and fluff with a fork. Season with salt, pepper, and more spice mixture, if desired. Sprinkle the pomegranate arils over the dish to garnish.

Skillet Pizza

Servings: 6   **Time:** 20 minutes

Ingredients

1 lb fresh pizza dough (store-bought or homemade), rolled to 14" diameter

1 tbsp olive oil, divided

2-3 cups mozzarella cheese, shredded

1 cup favorite marinara or pizza sauce

favorite pizza toppings

Directions

Heat skillet over low heat. Brush skillet with ½ tablespoon olive oil. This will help pizza get crispy. Lay dough in skillet and cook, uncovered, for 2-3 minutes until lightly browned.

Brush remaining oil on top of the dough and then flip over. Top with sauce, cheese, and toppings. Cover the skillet and cook for 4-6 minutes until cheese is melted. After a few minutes, check the bottom of the pizza. If it is browning too quickly, reduce heat to warm. Top with your favorite spices and serve.

Skillet Baked Ziti

Servings: 6-8 **Time:** 30 minutes

Ingredients

1 lb ziti

1 cup cream

3 (15 oz) cans crushed tomatoes

1 cup water

2 tbsp olive oil

1 onion, diced

1 tbsp dried oregano

½ tsp crushed red pepper flakes

½ tsp salt

2 cloves garlic, minced

8 oz ricotta cheese

12 oz mozzarella cheese, grated

¼ cup Parmesan cheese, grated

Directions

Place ziti in a bowl. Cover with hot water and season generously with salt. Let soak for at least 10 minutes, stirring occasionally.

Meanwhile, heat oil in the skillet over medium heat. Add the onion and sauté until translucent. Add garlic, oregano, red pepper flakes, and salt. Cook for 2 more minutes.

Mix tomatoes, cream, and water in a large bowl, mashing tomatoes slightly with a spatula or spoon. Season with salt and pepper and then add to skillet.

Drain the ziti and add to skillet. Stir in the ricotta cheese and half of the mozzarella. Cover the pasta with the remaining mozzarella and Parmesan cheese. Cover with lid and cook over low heat for 5 minutes. Turn off the skillet and let sit for 5-10 minutes before serving.

Spicy Sausage Penne

Servings: 4-6   **Time:** 30 minutes

Ingredients

1 lb spicy sausage, cut into 1" pieces

1 lb penne pasta

1 tbsp olive oil

4 cloves garlic, peeled and minced

2 (14 oz) cans diced tomatoes

2 tsp oregano

1 tsp red pepper flakes

1 medium yellow onion, diced

salt and pepper, to taste

Directions

Heat the oil over medium high heat. Sauté the sausage until cooked through. Drain most of the grease and set sausage aside.

Cook the onion for 5 minutes in remaining grease. Add minced garlic, oregano, and red pepper flakes. Cook another minute. Then, add diced tomatoes and cook for 15 minutes on low heat with the lid on. Meanwhile, cook penne according to package directions.

Add the sausage to the skillet and cook for another 5 minutes. Serve over penne pasta with Parmesan cheese.

Baked Tortellini

Servings: 6   **Time:** 30 minutes

Ingredients

1 (2 lbs) package refrigerated cheese tortellini

¼ cup butter

1 onion, sliced

2 cloves garlic, minced

6 cups spinach leaves

1 (15 oz) can diced fire-roasted tomatoes

1 (15 oz) can crushed tomatoes

1 tsp dried oregano

1 tsp dried basil

¼ tsp red pepper flakes

1 cup shredded mozzarella cheese, divided

salt and black pepper, to taste

Directions

Melt the butter in the skillet over medium heat. Add the onion, garlic, oregano, basil, red pepper flakes, and canned tomatoes. Cover and cook 10 minutes over medium low heat.

Add spinach and stir until slightly wilted. Then, mix in the tortellini.

Top with mozzarella cheese, cover, and cook for 15-20 minutes on low heat.

Serve hot.

Chicken & Orzo Skillet Casserole

Servings: 4   **Time:** 30 minutes

Ingredients

6 chicken thighs

2 tbsp olive oil

1 onion, chopped

1 bell pepper, chopped

2 cloves garlic, minced

1 tsp oregano

1 tsp onion powder

3 cups chicken broth

1½ cups orzo pasta

15 Kalamata olives, pits removed

1 lemon, cut into six wedges

¼ cup apricot jam

salt and pepper, to taste

Directions

Brown chicken in the olive oil over medium heat. Add chopped vegetables and sauté for about 5 minutes. Add remaining ingredients and season to taste.

Cover skillet and cook over medium heat for about 20 minutes, until the chicken is cooked through.

Chicken Schnitzel

Servings: 4   **Time:** 30 minutes

Ingredients

4 chicken cutlets, pounded to ⅓" thickness
2 eggs
2 cups whole-wheat flour
⅔ cup breadcrumbs
Italian seasoning, to taste
garlic powder, to taste
salt and pepper, to taste

Directions

Whisk the eggs in a large bowl. In a separate bowl, combine the breadcrumbs, Italian seasoning, garlic powder, salt, and pepper.

Spread flour on a plate. On a separate plate, spread the breadcrumb mixture.

Preheat the skillet over medium and lightly grease using oil of your choice. Dip chicken cutlets, one at a time, in the whole-wheat flour, then into the whisked egg, and finally into the breadcrumb mixture. Make sure to coat both sides of each cutlet.

Place in skillet and cook for about 7 minutes on each side or until cooked through.

Note: Cooking time may vary depending on thickness of the chicken. Make sure it is fully cooked before consuming.

Slim Geransar

"You can't go wrong with a Chicken Schnitzel! One of my family's all time favorites – especially as a child. Perfect when served with a simple salad and some guacamole."

Beef Quesadilla

Servings: 4 **Time:** 30 minutes

Ingredients

8 oz sirloin steak, cut into strips
¼ white onion, finely diced
1 cup grated cheese of your preference
4 whole wheat tortillas
salsa, avocado, and sour cream, to garnish
salt and pepper, to taste

Directions

Lightly grease the skillet. Cook onions over medium heat until lightly browned.

Add steak strips and season with salt and pepper. Cook until steak is done to your liking. Set aside.

Wipe skillet clean. Warm tortillas over medium low heat for about 20-30 seconds.

Flip tortillas and add cheese to one half of each tortilla. Once cheese has begun to melt, add steak and onions to the same side of each tortilla and fold in half so that the ends meet.

Serve with chunky salsa, diced avocado, and sour cream.

Beef Fajitas

Servings: 3-4 **Time:** 30 minutes

Ingredients

1 lb top sirloin steak, cut into thin strips
2 tbsp olive oil, divided
1 tbsp lime juice
2 garlic cloves, minced
½ tsp chili powder
½ tsp cumin
½ tsp smoked paprika
½ tsp crushed red pepper flakes (optional)
6-8 flour tortillas
½ red onion, sliced
1 red bell pepper, sliced
1 yellow bell pepper, sliced
2 tbsp cilantro, roughly chopped
1 cup salsa
salt and pepper, to taste
sour cream (optional)

Directions

In a bowl, combine 1 tablespoon olive oil, lime juice, garlic, chili powder, cumin, smoked paprika, red pepper flakes, salt, and pepper. Add steak and stir until coated. Set aside.

Warm tortillas individually in the skillet over medium low heat or wrapped together in foil in the oven at 300° for 5-10 minutes. Cover and keep tortillas warm in the oven until ready to use.

Heat remaining olive oil over medium heat. Add onions and peppers and cook for 3-4 minutes. Remove from skillet and set aside. Add steak to skillet and cook, stirring constantly until the steak is almost done to your liking. Add onions and peppers back to the skillet and continue cooking for a minute. Serve steak and vegetables over warmed tortillas and top with cilantro, salsa, and sour cream (optional).

32 one-pan kitchen

Meatball & Mozzarella Bake

Servings: 4-6   **Time:** 30 minutes

Ingredients

1 baguette

¼ cup (½ stick) butter

8 oz ricotta cheese

½ tsp of oregano

½ tsp salt

¼ cup Parmesan cheese, grated

1 lb meatballs (see recipe, page 166)

tomato sauce (see recipe, page 164)

2 cups mozzarella cheese, shredded

Directions

Slice the baguette so that the pieces fit into the skillet in one layer. Butter both sides and toast them in the skillet over medium heat. Turn off skillet.

Mix the ricotta, oregano, salt, and Parmesan cheese together and spread on top of the toasted baguettes. Top with meatballs.

Pour the tomato sauce over the meatballs and top with the mozzarella cheese. Place the lid on the skillet and cook on medium low until the meatballs are warmed through and the cheese is melted.

Cottage Cheese Pancakes   pg 40-41

Breakfast

36-37   Blueberry Yogurt Pancakes

38-39   Whole Wheat Pancakes

40-41   Cottage Cheese Pancakes

42-43   French Toast

44-45   Challah French Toast

46-47   Apple Cinnamon Breakfast Quinoa

48-49   Breakfast Hash

50-51   Tofu Scramble

Blueberry Yogurt Pancakes

Servings: 6–8   **Time:** 20 minutes

Ingredients

2 eggs

1 cup nonfat Greek yogurt

1½ cups milk

2 tbsp melted butter

1 tbsp superfine cane sugar

1 tsp salt

3 cups all-purpose or whole grain flour

1 cup fresh or frozen blueberries

Directions

Beat eggs in a bowl. Whisk in milk, melted butter, and Greek yogurt.

In a separate bowl, combine sugar, salt, and flour.

Add yogurt mixture to dry ingredients and mix until smooth. Fold in blueberries.

Preheat skillet over medium heat. Pour multiple ¼ cup pancakes onto skillet. Cook each side until golden brown.

Serve with maple syrup or a berry compote.

38 one-pan kitchen

Whole Wheat Pancakes

Servings: 4   **Time:** 20 minutes

Ingredients

2 eggs

2 cups milk

6 tbsp vegetable oil

2 cups whole wheat flour

1 cup unbleached all-purpose flour

4 tsp sugar

4 tsp baking powder

1 tsp salt

Directions

Mix all dry ingredients together in a bowl until well-combined. In a separate bowl, beat the eggs and then stir in the remaining liquids. Make a well in the dry ingredients and pour in the liquid mixture.

Mix the batter until most of the lumps are gone. Do not over mix.

Heat the skillet to medium or medium high heat. Pour the batter into several 4" circles on the skillet. Flip the pancakes once the center starts to bubble and the edges begin to dry out or appear firm.

Stack pancakes on a plate, drizzle with maple syrup, and serve.

40 one-pan kitchen

Cottage Cheese Pancakes

Servings: 4-6   **Time:** 20 minutes

Ingredients

1 cup cottage cheese

6 eggs, well beaten

6 tbsp all-purpose flour

6 tbsp canola, margarine, or butter, melted

Directions

Beat the cottage cheese with a whisk or hand mixer until smooth.

Add the remaining ingredients and beat until well combined.

Preheat skillet over medium or medium high heat. Lightly grease skillet and place the batter in big spoonfuls onto the cooking surface.

Cook until the bottoms are lightly browned and the edges look firm. Then flip to finish cooking the other side.

Rachel Hecht

"This is the recipe that my grandma and mom always cooked for me! They are so yummy!"

42   one-pan kitchen

French Toast

Servings: 4   **Time:** 20 minutes

Ingredients

8 thick slices of bread

4 eggs

½ cup milk or non-dairy milk alternative

1 tsp cinnamon

¼ tsp nutmeg

½ tsp vanilla extract

2 tbsp maple syrup or honey

¼ tsp salt

2-4 tbsp butter or oil, to grease pan

Directions

In a large bowl, whisk together eggs, milk, cinnamon, nutmeg, vanilla, maple syrup, and salt.

Place bread slices in a 9" x 13" pan. Pour egg mixture over bread and allow to soak for a few minutes. Then flip bread to coat both sides.

Melt butter on skillet over medium heat. Cook 4 slices of bread at a time until lightly browned on both sides.

Serve with maple syrup or a fruit compote.

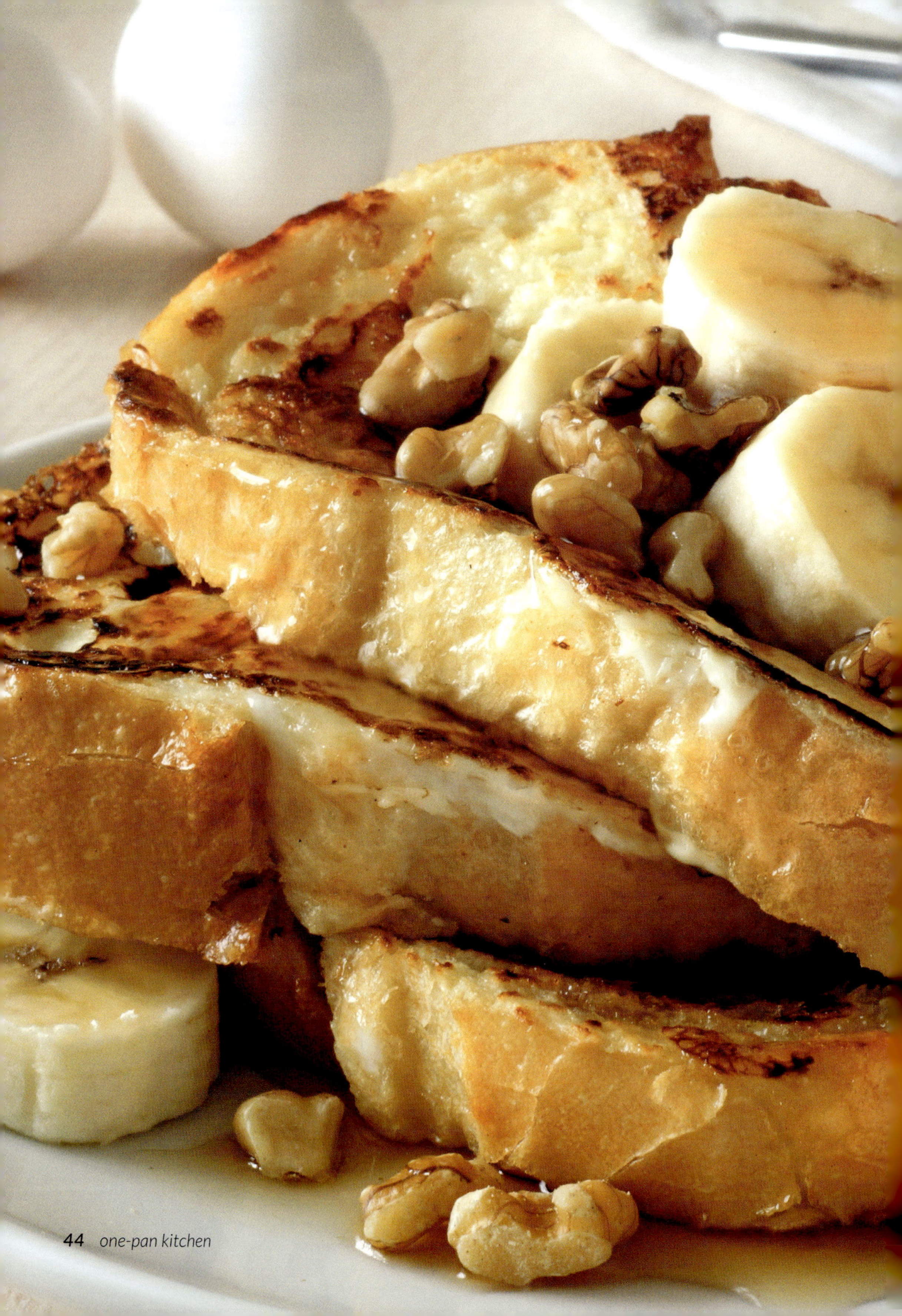

Challah French Toast

Servings: 4   **Time:** 25 minutes

Ingredients

1 loaf of Challah, sliced into 1" slices

6 eggs

½ cup whole milk

¼ tsp salt

2 bananas, sliced

½ cup walnuts

½ cup maple syrup

4 tbsp salted butter, divided

Directions

Slice the Challah and leave the slices out overnight to dry out. You can also use an old loaf that has become hard for this recipe.

Preheat the skillet on low with 2 tablespoons of butter. Mix together the eggs, milk, and salt with a hand mixer. Dip each slice of Challah into the mix and then put it directly onto the hot pan. When all of the slices are in the pan, cover and cook for 3-4 minutes. Uncover the skillet and flip the slices using a spatula. Cook for an additional 3-4 minutes. Flip once more and cook for 1 minute.

Serve with sliced bananas, the remaining butter, maple syrup, and walnuts.

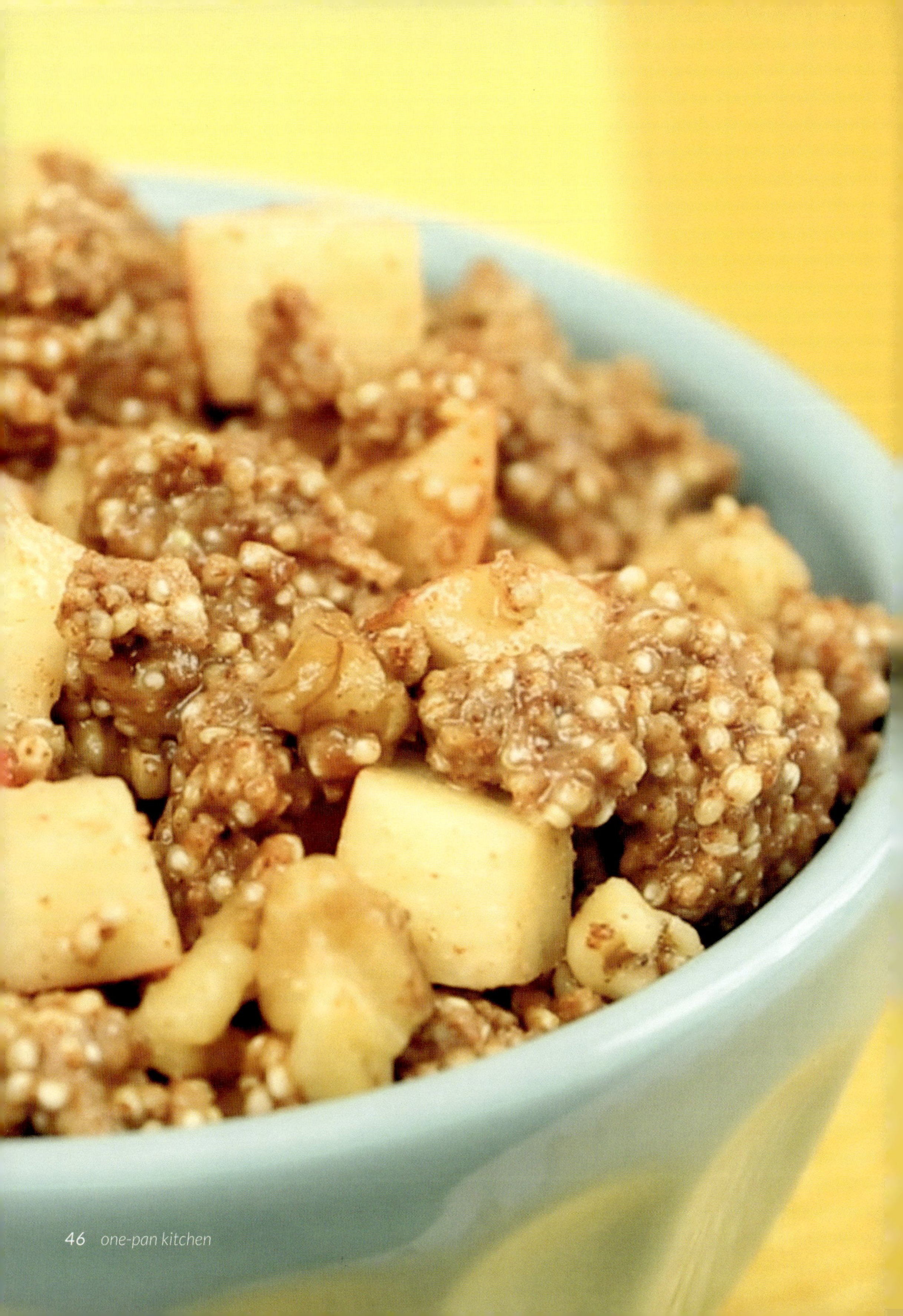

Apple Cinnamon Breakfast Quinoa

Servings: 8   **Time:** 25 minutes

Ingredients

2 cups quinoa

4 cups milk or almond milk

2 diced apples

1 cup almond buttter

2 tbsp cinnamon

honey, to drizzle

Directions

Rinse quinoa thoroughly and place in skillet. Add milk and cook in skillet over high heat.

When mixture reaches a boil, reduce to low heat, cover, and let simmer until fully cooked according to package instructions.

After quinoa is cooked, remove from skillet and fluff with fork. Mix in almond butter and cinnamon. Allow to cool for 10 minutes.

Mix in diced apples. Top with your favorite nuts and drizzle with honey.

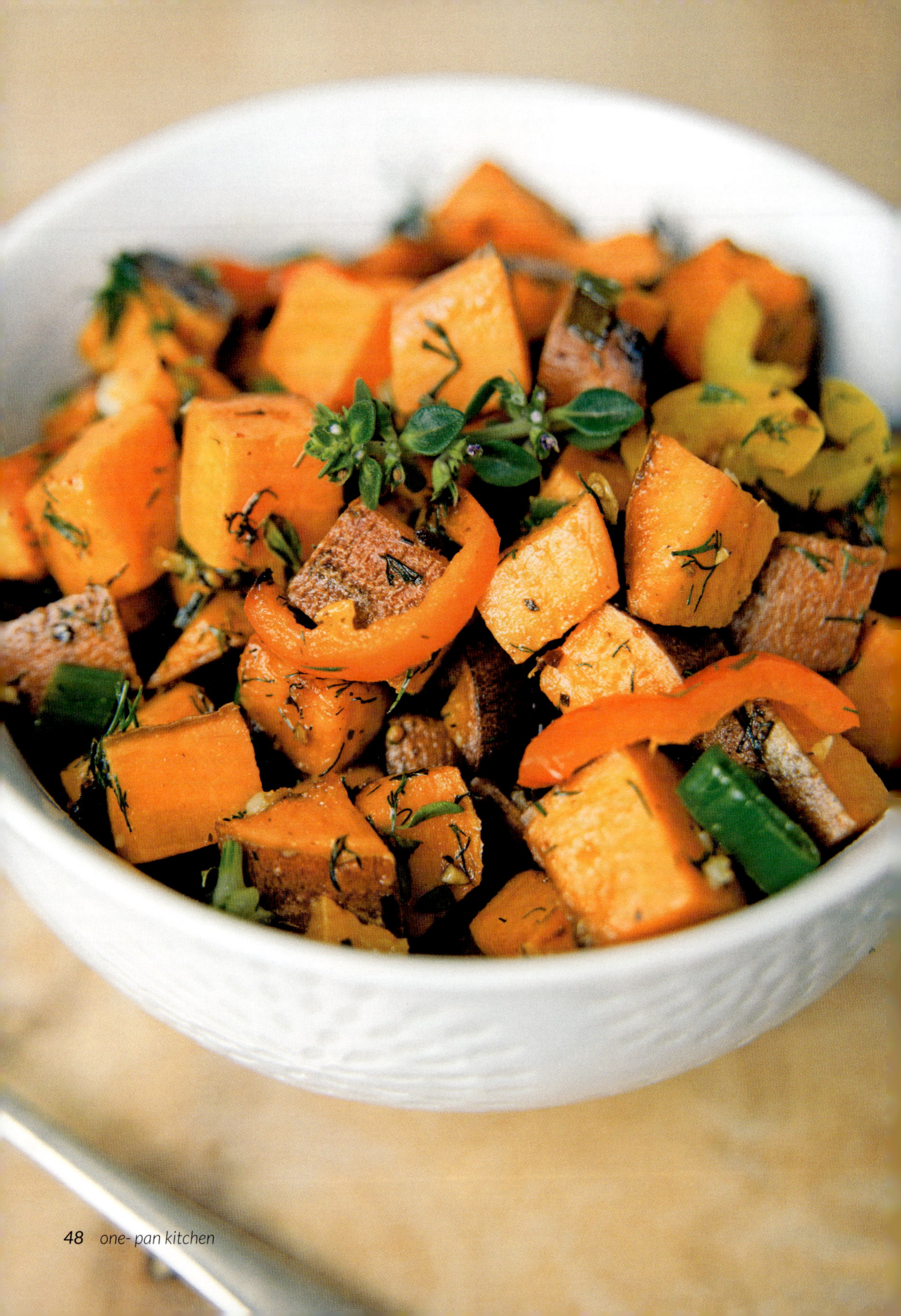

Breakfast Hash

Servings: 4-6   **Time:** 25 minutes

Ingredients

6 slices thick cut bacon

6 eggs

4 medium sweet potatoes, peeled and cubed

1 green pepper, diced

1 red pepper, diced

1 medium onion, diced

1 tsp fresh thyme

1 tsp salt

1 tsp pepper

Directions

Heat skillet over medium and lay bacon flat in the pan. Cook, turning once until crisp (about 2 minutes on each side). Remove bacon from skillet but leave any rendered fat.

Reduce heat to low. Add sweet potatoes, peppers, and onion. Sprinkle with thyme, salt, and pepper. Stir to combine. Spread to make an even layer and let cook for 2-3 minutes without stirring. Stir to redistribute the ingredients and spread into an even layer again. Let cook for 2-3 minutes. Add bacon and repeat this process once more.

Use a silicone spoon to create 6 small holes in the hash and crack one egg into each indentation. Cover with the lid and let cook for 6-8 minutes or until the egg whites are set.

50 one- pan kitchen

Tofu Scramble

Servings: 2-4 **Time:** 20 minutes

Ingredients

1 lb extra firm tofu, cut into 1" cubes

1 bunch of spinach or kale, coarsely chopped

6-8 crimini mushrooms, thinly sliced

1 garlic clove, minced

2 tbsp olive oil

1 tbsp soy sauce

1 tbsp nutritional yeast

1 tsp chili flakes, to garnish

salt and pepper, to taste

Directions

Heat olive oil over medium heat. Once the pan is hot, place the tofu on the skillet in one layer. Add soy sauce, nutritional yeast, salt, and pepper. Stir to coat the tofu.

Cook tofu for 10 minutes or until the tofu is crispy on the outside. Add garlic, spinach, and mushroom to pan. Stir until spinach is slightly wilted and mushrooms are cooked through.

Garnish with chili flakes and serve.

If using kale instead of spinach, add the kale with the tofu to the pan, keeping tofu and kale separate, and cook both for 15 minutes.

Julian Master

"I love making this tofu scramble because it's quick to make and healthy. I grew up in a vegan household and my mom used to make it for breakfast before I went to school. It goes well with a thick piece of toasted sourdough bread and chili hot sauce on the side."

breakfast

Butternut Squash & Sage Frittata   pg 66-67

Eggs

54-55   Spanish Omelette

56-57   Steak and Egg Breakfast Wrap

58   Blissful Breakfast Scramble

59   Southwest Breakfast Scramble

60-61   Spinach Egg White Omelette

62-63   Cheese Strata

64-65   Basic Frittata

66-67   Butternut Squash & Sage Frittata

68-69   Tuscan Fritatta

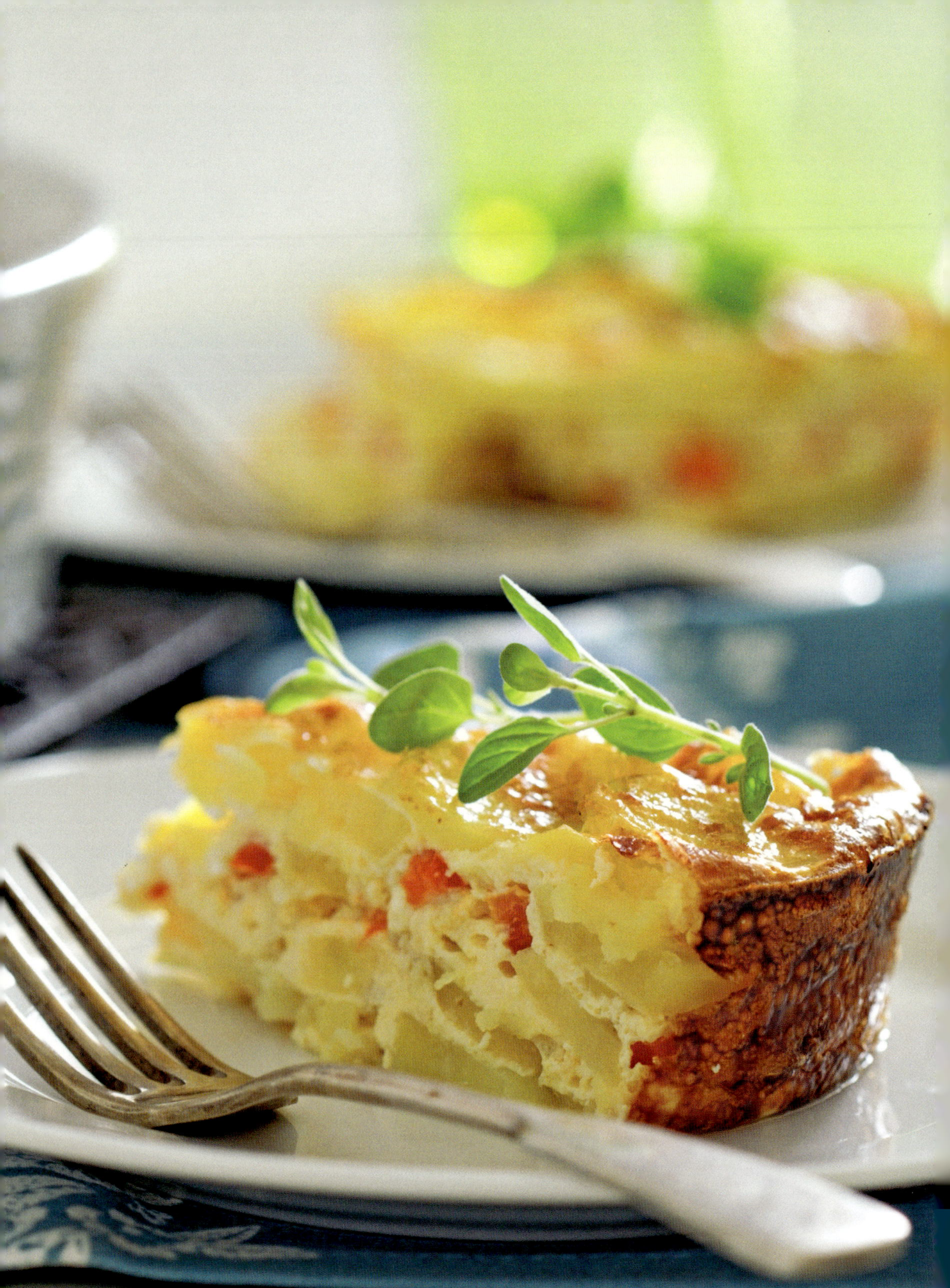

Spanish Omelette

Servings: 6   **Time:** 40 minutes

Ingredients

12 eggs

2 tbsp water

2 tbsp olive oil

2 medium red potatoes, thinly sliced

1 red bell pepper, diced

1 yellow onion, diced

salt and pepper, to taste

Directions

Sauté the onion and bell pepper in olive oil on medium heat in the skillet for 2 minutes. Then, add potatoes and season with salt and pepper. Cook another 5-8 minutes or until potatoes are cooked through.

Whisk together eggs and 2 tablespoons of water. Season with salt and pepper.

Pour egg mixture over vegetables and cook for 2 minutes on medium heat. Then, reduce the heat to low and cook for 15 minutes uncovered. Cover and cook for 5 more minutes until eggs are firm on top and lightly browned on the bottom.

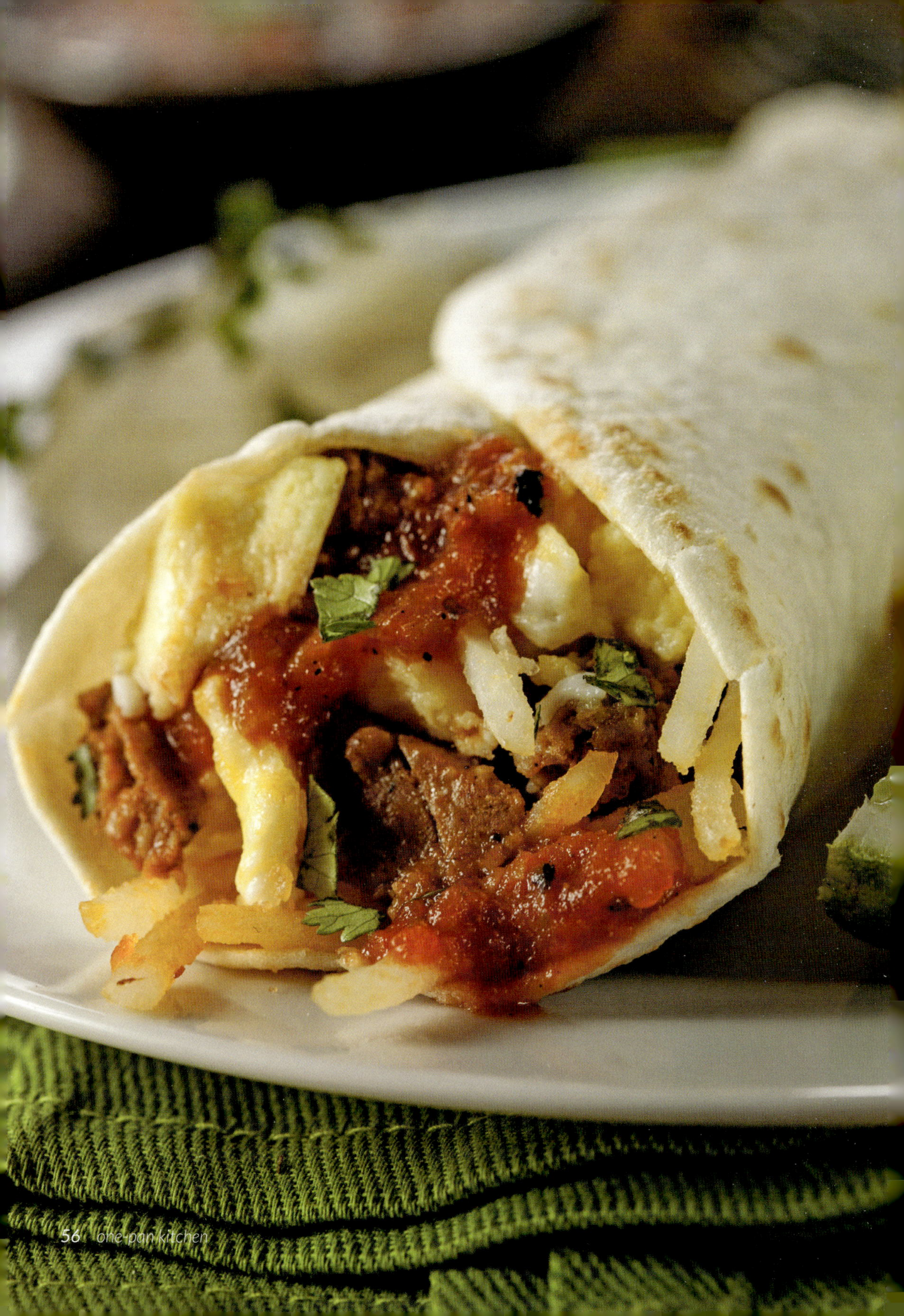

Steak and Egg Breakfast Wrap

Servings: 4   **Time:** 25 minutes

Ingredients

8 eggs

1 cup cheese, shredded

8 oz steak, cubed

4 (10") whole wheat tortillas

½ cup chunky salsa

salt and pepper, to taste

mixed greens (optional)

2 green onions, chopped (optional)

Directions

Beat eggs in a large bowl until frothy. Add cheese, salt, and pepper.

Heat the skillet over medium low heat and cook eggs until they are done but not dry. Set aside. Lightly oil skillet and cook steak as desired.

Spoon eggs, steak, salsa, mixed greens, and green onions onto the tortillas. Roll tightly and enjoy.

Blissful Breakfast Scramble

Servings: 6–8   **Time:** 35 minutes

Ingredients

2 dozen eggs

2 baked sweet potatoes, diced

2 cups of mushrooms

2 cups spinach

2 yellow onions, thinly sliced

½ cup sharp cheddar cheese, shredded

2 tbsp butter, divided

Directions

Heat 1 tablespoon of butter in the skillet on low and cook the onions for about 10 minutes, stirring frequently until they begin to develop a golden brown color.

Whisk the eggs in a large bowl.

Add the mushrooms, spinach, and baked sweet potatoes to the pan and cook for 1 minute. Add the eggs and the remaining butter to the pan. Sprinkle the cheese over the eggs and begin to gently stir. Cook over low heat, stirring constantly until eggs are almost set.

Southwest Breakfast Scramble

Servings: 6-8   **Time:** 35 minutes

Ingredients

2 dozen eggs

6 oz chorizo, casing removed

1 medium red onion, diced

½ red bell pepper, diced

½ green bell pepper, diced

½ cup frozen or pre-cooked corn kernels

½ cup canned black beans

1 cup cheddar or Monterey Jack cheese, shredded

¾ cup green onion, to garnish

½ cup sour cream, to garnish

Directions

Cook the chorizo in the pan over medium heat. Lower the heat and add the diced onion and bell peppers. Cook for 2 minutes. Add the corn and black beans and cook for 1-2 additional minutes.

Whisk the eggs in a large bowl.

Pour in the eggs. Sprinkle the cheese over the eggs and begin to gently stir the mixture with a spatula over low heat. Serve with a dollop of sour cream and chopped green onion.

60   one-pan kitchen

Spinach Egg White Omelette

Servings: 2   **Time:** 15-20 minutes

Ingredients

5 egg whites

1 cup fresh spinach

3 tsp olive oil, divided

fresh parsley

grated Romano cheese (optional)

salt and pepper, to taste

Directions

Sauté the spinach in 2 tablespoons olive oil on low to medium heat. Remove from pan and set aside. Whisk the egg whites in a bowl. Stir in the parsley. Set your skillet to low so that it is warm, not hot.

Coat the skillet with remaining oil. Pour in the egg mixture. After the egg has begun to cook, lay the cooked spinach on top of the eggs.

With a spatula, gently lift and fold the right side of the omelette over the other side. Softly press the omelette down. Top with a little cheese and season with salt and pepper.

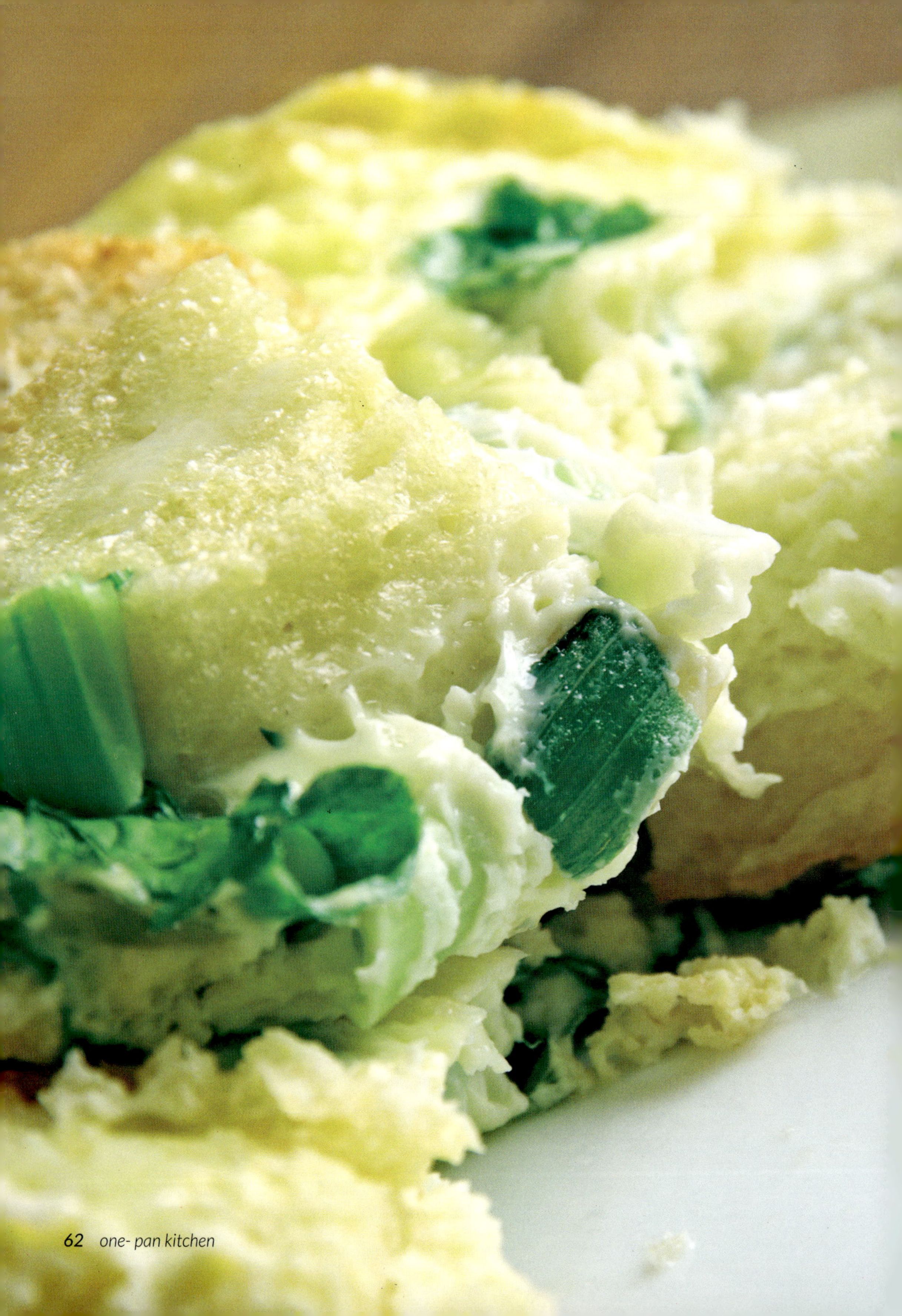

Cheese Strata

Servings: 4   **Time:** 40 minutes

Ingredients

12 large eggs

2½ cups milk

½ tsp salt

¼ tsp black pepper

6 1" thick slices of bread, crusts removed

4 green onions, chopped

6 oz Monterey Jack cheese, grated

6 oz mozzarella cheese, shredded

Directions

Butter the skillet. In a medium bowl, mix together milk, eggs, salt, and pepper. Cover bottom of pan with bread. Sprinkle half the cheese and half the green onion over the bread. Place another layer of bread on top and fill in gaps with extra bread.

Cover with the rest of the cheese and green onion. Pour the egg and milk mixture over the top of the bread. Cover with the lid and turn the heat to medium low.

Cook the strata for 20-30 minutes or until it puffs and the cheese is melted.

one-pan kitchen

Basic Frittata

Servings: 4   **Time:** 35 minutes

Ingredients

6 eggs

¼ cup Parmesan cheese, grated

¼ cup sour cream

¼ tsp black pepper

½ tsp salt

1 tbsp butter

½ green bell pepper, chopped

½ orange bell pepper, chopped

½ cup ham, diced

Directions

Whisk together the eggs, sour cream, salt, pepper, and Parmesan cheese. Melt butter in the skillet on medium heat.

Sauté the ham and bell peppers for 5 minutes.

Pour eggs over the ham and vegetables and reduce heat to low. Cook frittata with the lid on until puffy and browned on the sides, about 20 minutes.

Butternut Squash & Sage Frittata

Servings: 10　　**Time:** 45 minutes

Ingredients

24 eggs

1 cup milk

10-15 sage leaves

1 cup Parmesan cheese, grated

2 tbsp olive oil

2 cloves garlic, minced

1 butternut squash, peeled and cubed

1 yellow onion, chopped

½ cup canned peas (optional)

sea salt, to taste

fresh ground pepper, to taste

Directions

Heat 2 tablespoons olive oil in skillet on medium heat. Once hot, add sage and toss. Fry until the sage is crispy but not brown. Remove sage from pan and set aside on a paper towel. Sprinkle with sea salt. Crumble the sage once it has cooled.

In large bowl, whisk eggs, milk, garlic, ¼ teaspoon of salt, freshly ground pepper, and half of the Parmesan cheese.

In skillet, add onion over medium heat. Stir to coat the onions and cook until translucent. Add butternut squash and a pinch of sea salt. Stir and cover. Reduce heat to low to avoid burning. Cook until butternut squash is fork tender.

Uncover and raise temperature to cook off excess moisture. Cook until the butternut squash starts to turn golden brown (about 5 minutes).

Melissa Holmes

"I love having butternut squash with dinner and this is a great way to use the same ingredients from the night before for breakfast! It's the perfect blend of sweet and savory."

Directions continued

Reduce heat. Spread butternut squash evenly on bottom of skillet. Whisk egg mixture one last time and add to skillet along with the peas. Sprinkle with remaining cheese. Cover and cook for about 15-20 minutes until the middle of the egg mixture is barely set (shake the pan to test).

Once set, sprinkle with a pinch of sea salt and crumbled sage. Let sit for a few minutes.

Slice and serve.

68   one-pan kitchen

Tuscan Fritatta

Servings: 10 **Time:** 35 minutes

Ingredients

2 dozen eggs

1 cup ham, chopped

3 tbsp olive oil

2 small yellow onions, diced

2 cloves garlic, minced

¼ cup marinated olives

2 cups kale, finely chopped

1 cup roasted red peppers, thinly sliced

1 cup roasted asparagus, chopped

½ cup Parmigiano Reggiano, grated

1 cup fontina or semisoft cheese, shredded

salt and pepper, to taste

Directions

Sauté the onions in garlic and olive oil over low heat. Add kale and cook for 1-2 minutes. Then, add roasted red peppers, roasted asparagus, ham, and olives to the pan. Cook for 1-2 minutes.

In a large bowl, beat the eggs until they are fluffy. Mix in the cheeses. Pour the egg and cheese mixture over the fillings and season with salt and pepper. Cover and cook on low for about 8-10 minutes or until the top of the frittata is set. Check frequently to make sure the bottom is not burning. Cook for additonal time, if necessary.

Slice into wedges and serve warm. This frittata can also be frozen and reheated for a quick, easy meal.

Honey BBQ Wings pg 76-77

Appetizers

72-73	Game Day Nachos
74-75	Classic Buffalo Wings
76-77	Honey BBQ Wings
78-79	Sesame Ginger Wings
80-81	Yucca Fritters
82-83	Bacon Wrapped Dates
84-85	Spinach Pizza
86-87	Greek Pizza
88-89	Cranberry Meatballs
90-91	Tomato Spinach & Mozzarella Wrap
92-93	Chicken Quesadillas
94-95	Spinach and Artichoke Dip
96-97	Queso Dip
98-99	Garlic Crostini

72   one-pan kitchen

Game Day Nachos

Servings: 6–8   **Time:** 20 minutes

Ingredients

8 oz flank steak, cubed

1½ cups cheddar cheese, finely grated

1 tbsp olive oil

1 avocado, diced

2 tomatoes, diced

¼ cup chopped cilantro

1 lime

1 (13 oz) bag tortilla chips

salt and pepper, to taste

Directions

In the skillet, sauté the flank steak in the olive oil on medium heat until cooked to your liking. Season with salt and pepper and set aside.

Over medium heat, layer chips, cheese, and steak in the skillet. Place the lid on the skillet and allow the nachos to heat and the cheese to melt. Turn the heat off and top with avocado, tomatoes, cilantro, and fresh lime juice.

For entertaining, we recommend doubling this recipe.

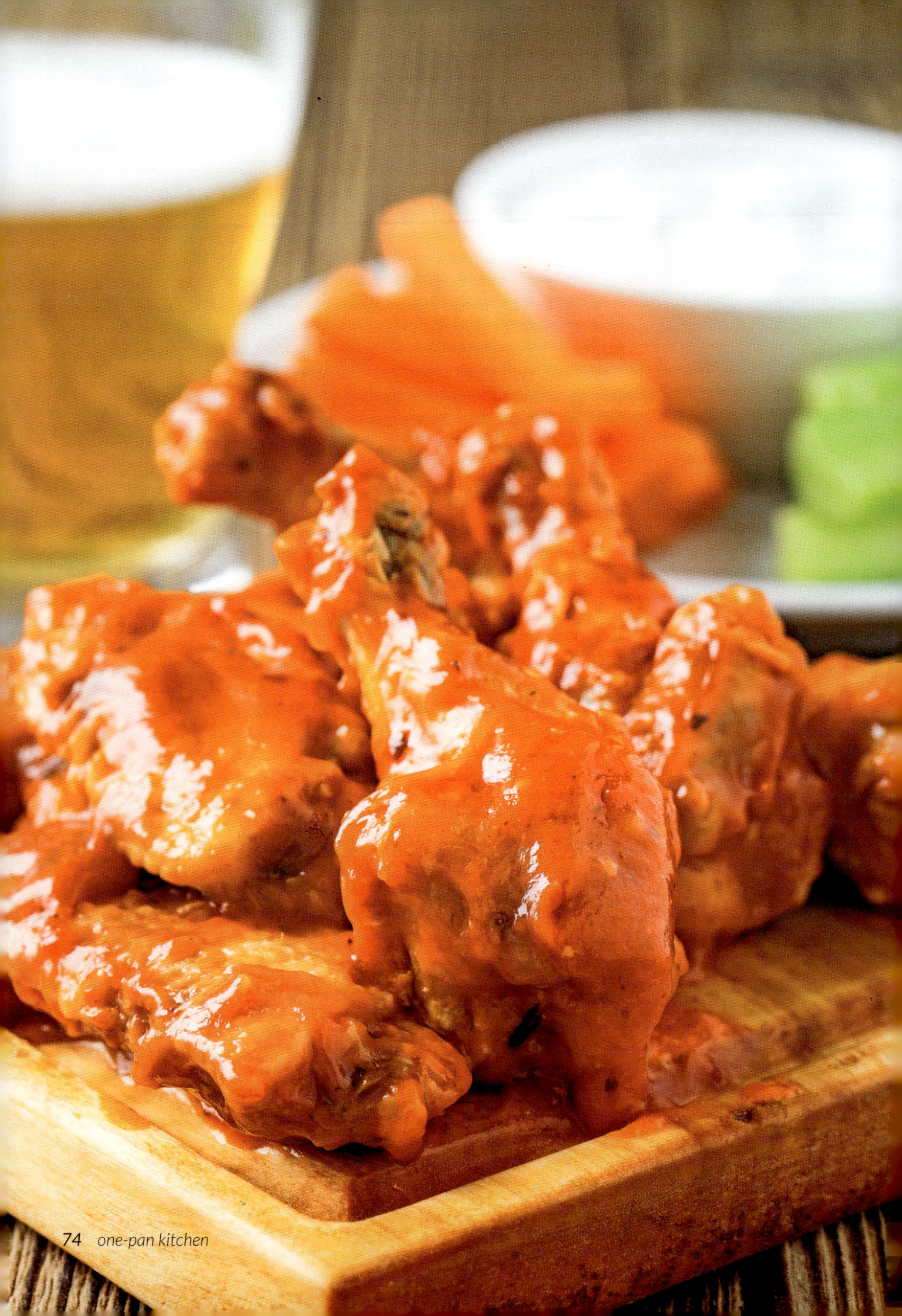

Classic Buffalo Wings

Servings: 6-8   **Time:** 40 minutes

Ingredients

24 chicken wings (2-3 lbs)
¾ cup all-purpose flour
1 tsp salt
2 tsp paprika
¾ cup hot sauce
5 tbsp butter, melted
1 tsp Worcestershire sauce
8 cups vegetable oil

Directions

Heat oil in the skillet until it shimmers or until a thermometer reads 350°F. Mix the salt, paprika, and flour together in a shallow bowl. Dip each chicken wing in the flour mixture. Add the wings to the hot oil.

Cook wings for 10-15 minutes, turning every few minutes to ensure they brown evenly.

Set wings on a paper towel lined plate to drain excess oil.

In a large bowl, mix the hot sauce, Worcestershire sauce, and butter together. Toss the wings in the sauce and serve.

one-pan kitchen

Honey BBQ Wings

Servings: 6-8   **Time:** 40 minutes

Ingredients

24 chicken wings (2-3 lbs)
¾ cup all-purpose flour
1 tsp salt
2 tsp paprika
½ cup honey
½ cup BBQ sauce
¼ cup soy sauce
8 cups vegetable oil

Directions

In the skillet, heat honey, BBQ sauce, and soy sauce. Simmer for about 5 minutes. Set sauce aside.

Heat oil in the skillet until it shimmers or until a thermometer reads 350°F.

Mix the salt, paprika, and flour together in a shallow bowl. Dip each chicken wing in the flour and salt mixture. Add the wings to the hot oil.

Cook wings for 10-15 minutes, turning every few minutes to ensure they brown evenly. Place wings on paper towels to drain excess oil.

Discard oil. Return wings to pan over medium heat. Pour honey BBQ sauce over wings and toss to coat. Cook until sauce begins to caramelize.

appetizers

78 one-pan kitchen

Sesame Ginger Wings

Servings: 6-8   **Time:** 40 minutes

Ingredients

24 chicken wings (2-3 lbs)

¾ cup all-purpose flour

1 tsp salt

1 tsp ground ginger

½ cup honey

½ cup soy sauce

2 tbsp hoisin sauce

2 cloves garlic, minced

2 tsp fresh ginger, grated

3 tbsp white sesame seeds

2 green onions, to garnish

8 cups vegetable oil

Directions

In the skillet, toast the sesame seeds until aromatic. Set aside. Heat honey, hoisin sauce, soy sauce, ginger, and garlic in the skillet. Simmer for about 5 minutes. Set sauce aside.

Heat oil in the skillet until it shimmers or until a thermometer reads 350°F. Mix the salt, ground ginger, and flour together in a shallow bowl. Dip each chicken wing in the flour and salt mixture. Add the wings to the hot oil.

Cook wings for 10-15 minutes, turning every few minutes to ensure they brown evenly. Set wings on paper towels to drain. Toss the wings in the ginger sauce and sprinkle with toasted sesame seeds. Garnish with chopped green onion if desired.

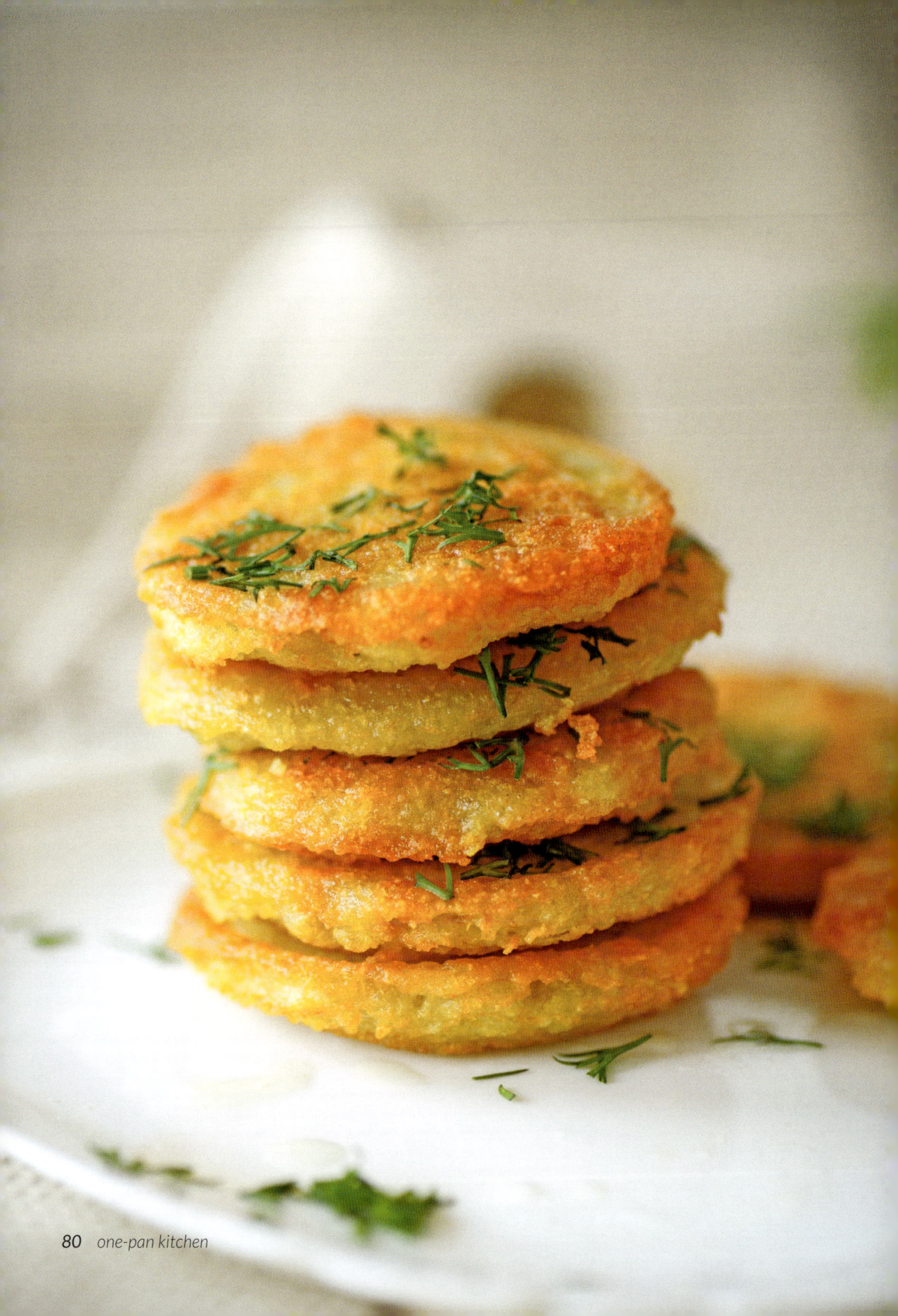

Yucca Fritters

Servings: 4-6   **Time:** 30 minutes

Ingredients

2 lbs Yucca, peeled and grated

2 eggs

¼ tsp sugar

½ tsp anise seed

8 cups oil (canola or grapeseed)

Directions

In a mixing bowl, mix the yucca, eggs, sugar, and anise seed until well incorporated.

Form into patties.

Heat the oil in the skillet over high heat. Make sure that the oil has a high smoke point. Gently drop the Yucca patties into the frying pan one by one, taking care not to splash any oil.

Fry until the patties are just golden. Flip to cook the other side and then place on paper towels to drain.

Giselle Regino

"Aside from enjoying how this recipe tastes, I love this recipe because it reminds me of eating amazing food at my mother's house."

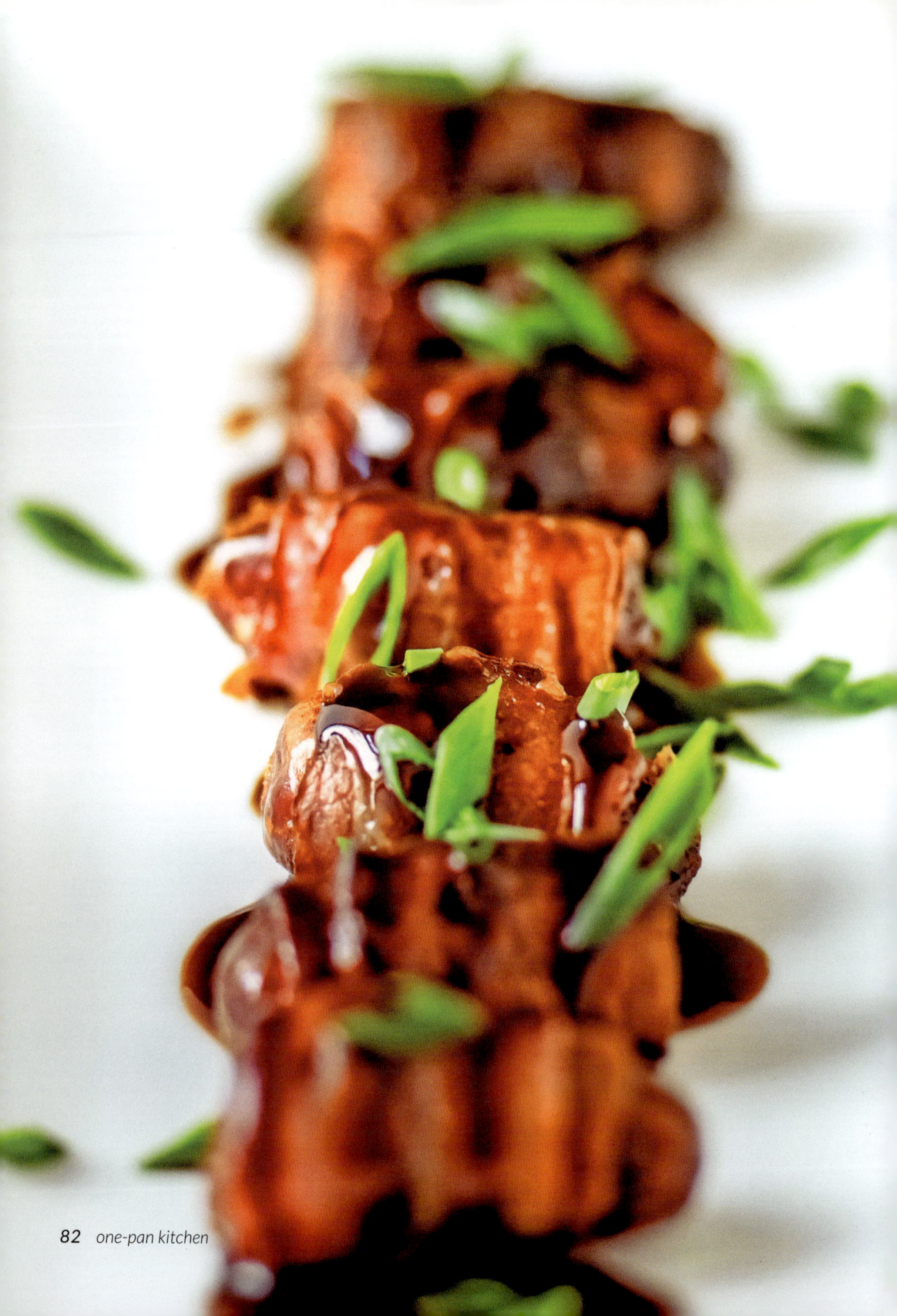

Bacon Wrapped Dates

Servings: 8   **Time:** 20 minutes

Ingredients

16 pitted dates

8 slices bacon, cut in half

32 roasted almonds

balsamic vinegar, to drizzle

Directions

Push two almonds into each date and wrap with a half piece of bacon. Secure the bacon with a toothpick.

Place dates in the skillet on medium high heat and cook, rotating to ensure all the bacon gets crispy.

Serve with a drizzle of balsamic vinegar.

This recipe can also be made with blue cheese stuffed dates.

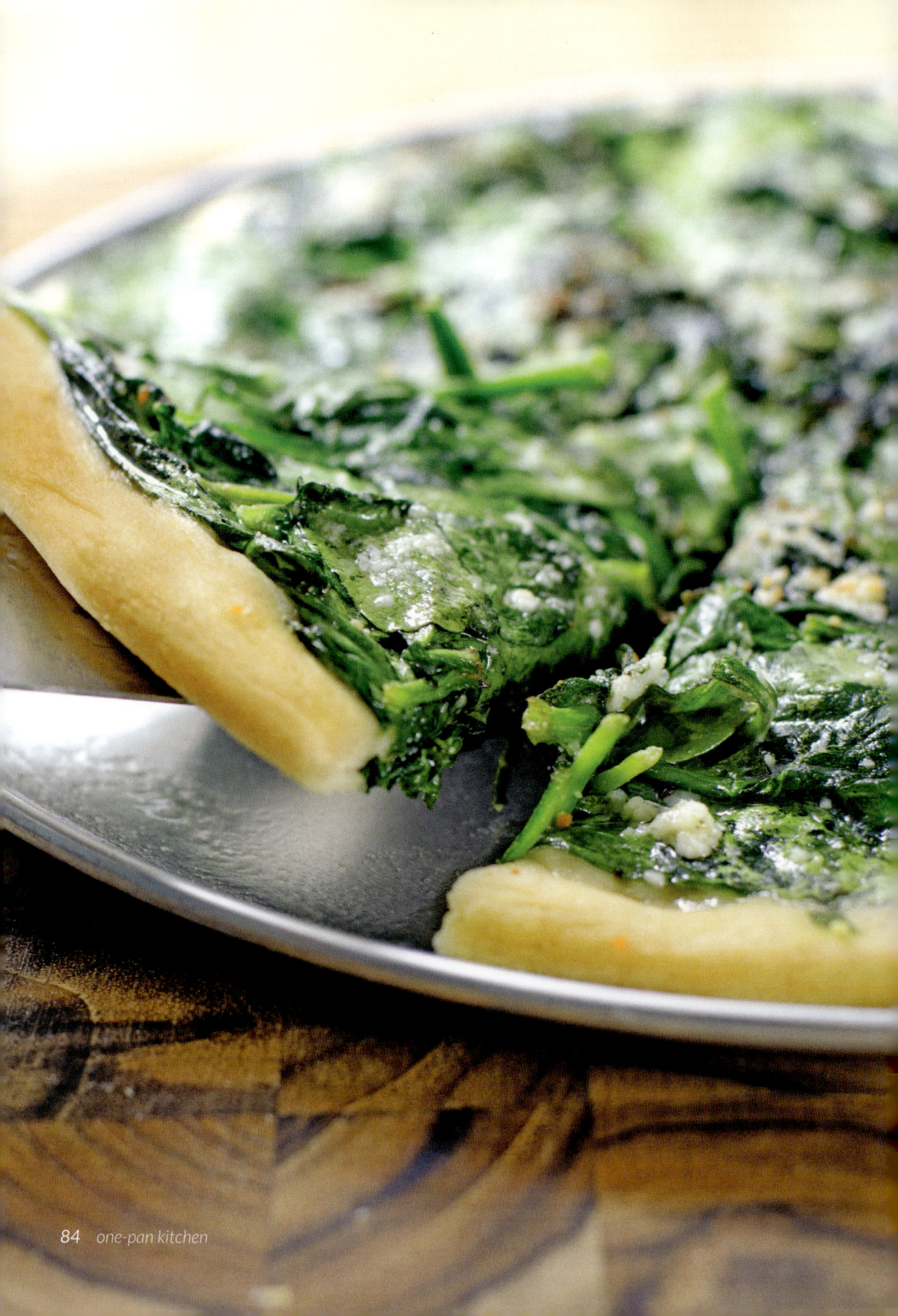

Spinach Pizza

Servings: 8-10   **Time:** 15 minutes

Ingredients

1 homemade or store-bought pizza dough

2 tbsp grated Pecorino Romano cheese

12 oz fresh baby spinach, washed

3½ tbsp olive oil, divided

1 large garlic clove, crushed

pinch of salt

¼ tsp coarse ground black pepper

Directions

Mix garlic, 2 tablespoons olive oil, salt, and pepper in a large bowl. Add spinach. Shake the cheese over the spinach and toss well.

Roll dough into a circle with a 14" diameter. Turn skillet to low and brush bottom of dough with 1 tablespoon oil.

Place dough in the skillet so that the oiled side is face-down and cook, uncovered, for about 3-4 minutes until bottom is lightly browned. Brush top of dough with ½ tbsp olive oil and flip it over.

Spread spinach topping evenly over the pizza dough. Sprinkle a little more cheese and olive oil over the pizza.

Cover and cook for 4-6 minutes. Check bottom and, if browning too quickly, reduce heat to warm. Allow to cool slightly. Remove pizza from skillet and cut with a pizza cutter to serve.

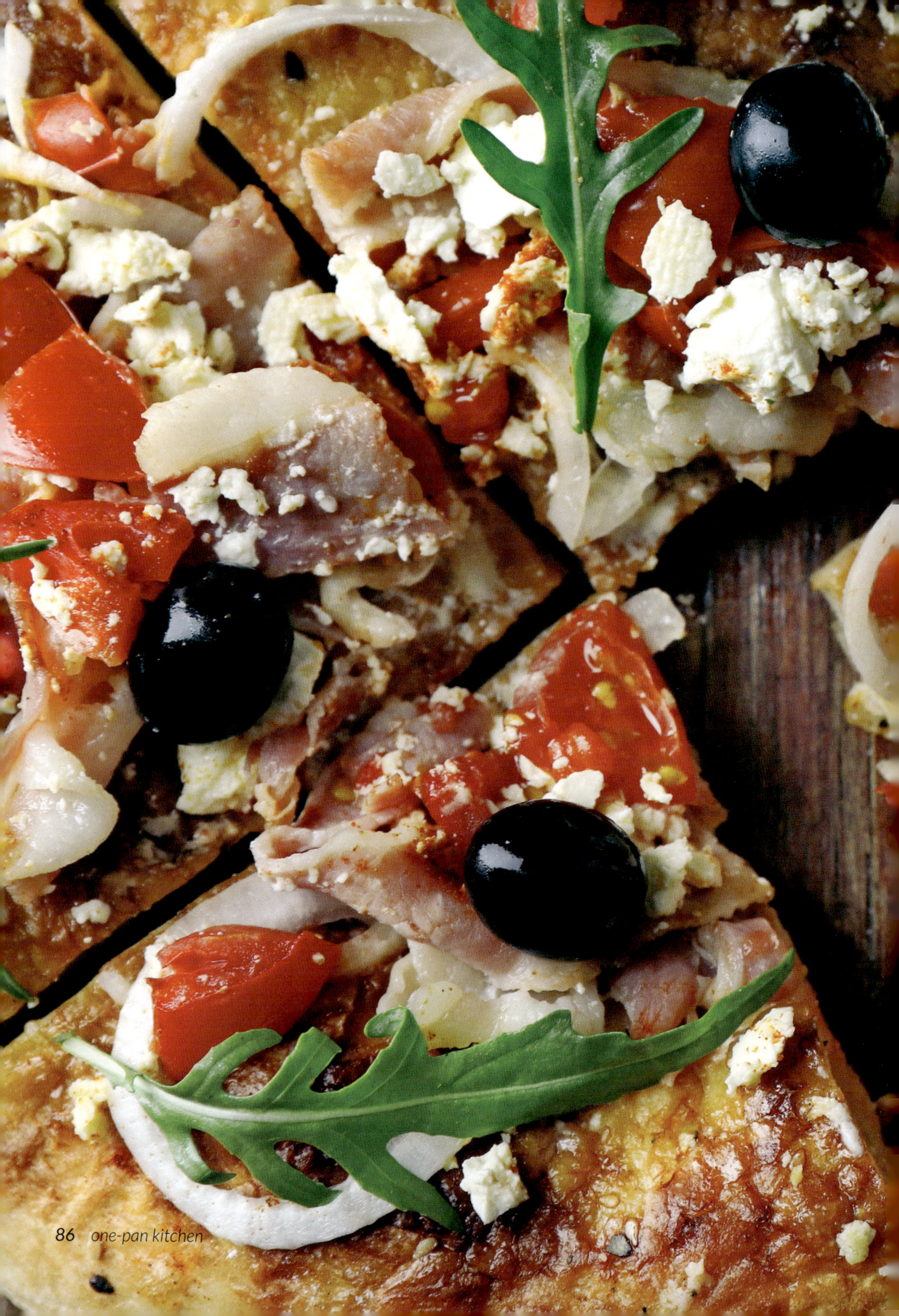

Greek Pizza

Servings: 8   **Time:** 45 minutes

Ingredients

Pizza dough:

1½ cups unbleached flour

1 tsp yeast

1 tsp salt

¾ cup cold water

2 tbsp olive oil

Toppings:

10 Kalamata olives, pitted

8 slices fresh salami

fresh arugula

¼ cup red onion, sliced

4 oz fresh feta cheese

Directions

To make the pizza dough: mix half the flour and the rest of the dry ingredients in the bowl of a stand mixer with the paddle attachment.

Add the cold water while the machine is on low and mix for 1 minute. Add the rest of the flour and mix together. Increase the speed of the machine to high and continue to mix for 4-6 minutes.

Cover and leave on counter for at least an hour. Punch down dough and roll out to fit the skillet. Poke all over with a fork. Let it rest for 15 minutes. Place 1 tablespoon olive oil in the skillet and place the pizza dough on top. Cook for 5 minutes, uncovered, until the bottom is crisp.

Brush top of dough with remaining olive oil and flip the pizza over. Cover with all the toppings except arugula. Cover and cook for 10 minutes or until the dough is cooked through and the cheese is completely melted. Top with arugula and serve.

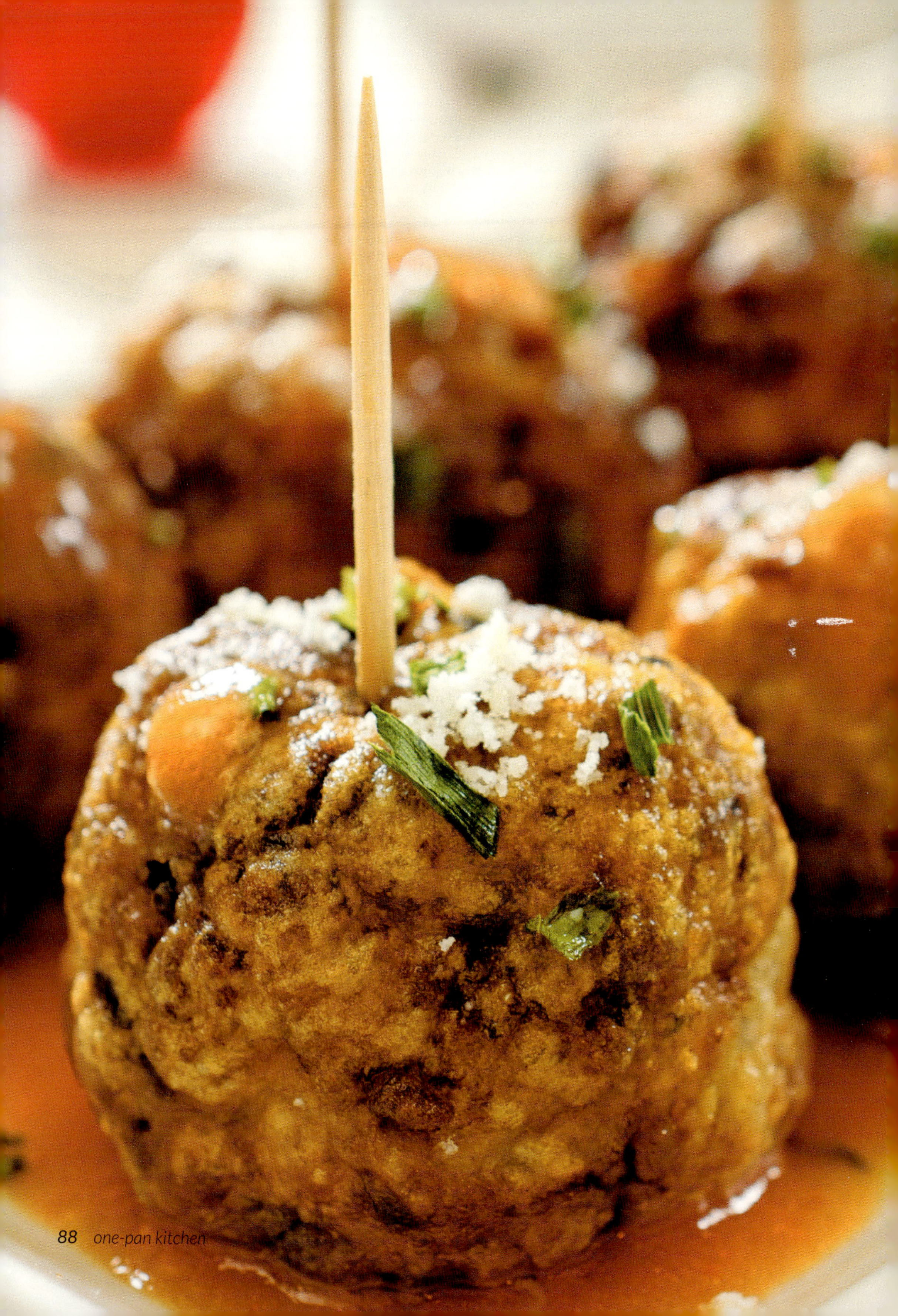

Cranberry Meatballs

Servings: 8-12   **Time:** 1½ hours

Ingredients

2 lbs ground beef

2 eggs

1 (12 oz) bottle chili sauce

1 (14 oz) can jellied cranberry

1 cup breadcrumbs

½ small onion, chopped finely

2 tbsp brown sugar

1 tbsp oil

salt and pepper, to taste

Directions

Mix the beef, eggs, breadcrumbs, onion, salt, and pepper in a medium bowl. Roll the meat into meatballs the size of a quarter.

Drizzle oil in skillet and brown the meatballs. Remove the meatballs from the skillet, drain, and clean.

In the skillet, mix the chili sauce, jellied cranberry, and brown sugar. Stir the sauce until smooth. Return the meatballs to the skillet and cover. Turn the skillet to low.

Bake for 1 hour. Let the meatballs cool for 15 minutes before serving.

Elizabeth Skinner

"This is a recipe from my dad's side of the family and has become a party favorite. The cranberry sauce provides a sweet twist to the ordinary meatball."

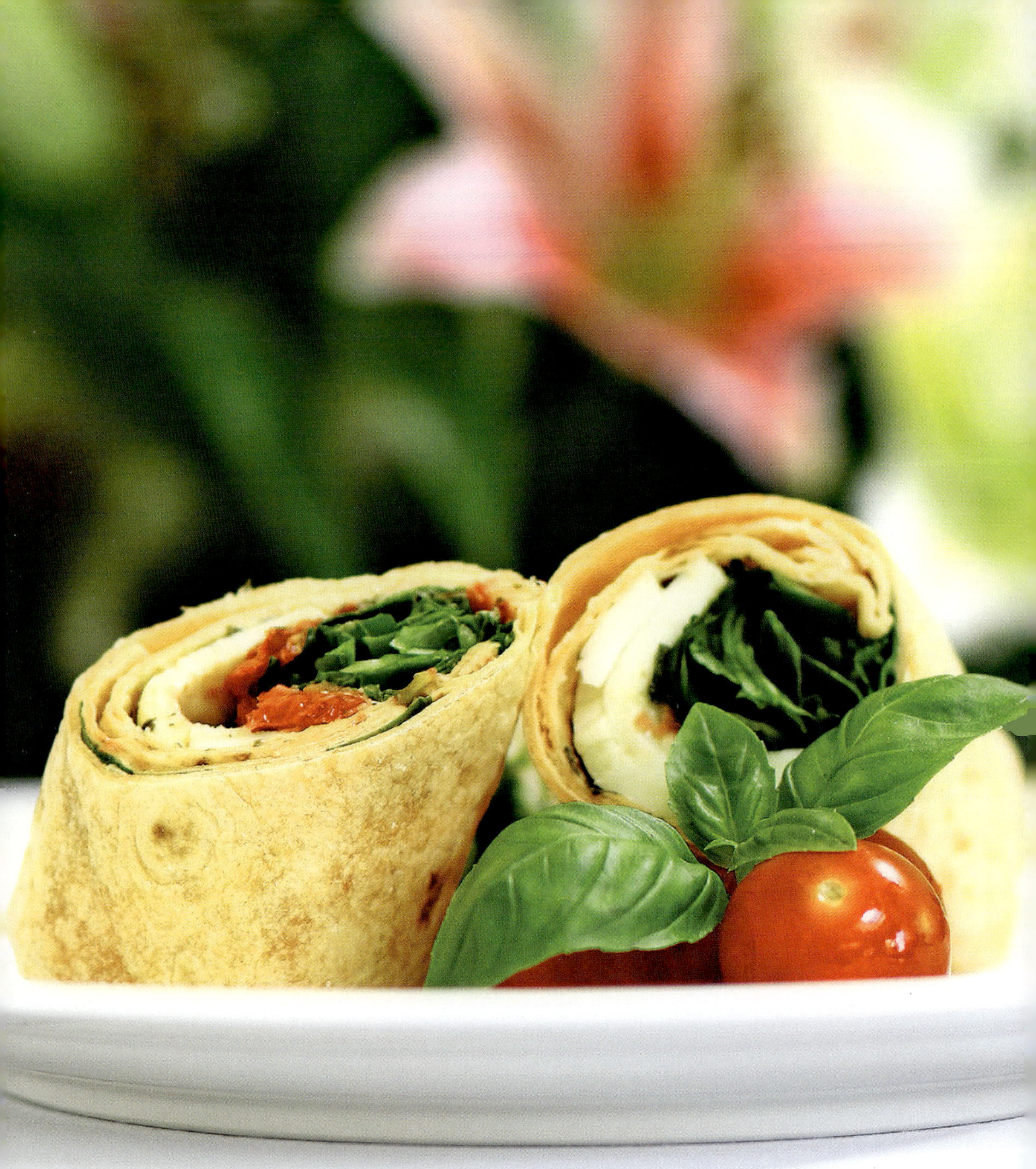

Tomato Spinach & Mozzarella Wrap

Servings: 4   **Time:** 15- 20 minutes

Ingredients

4 whole wheat tortillas

8 eggs

1 cup fresh mozzarella, shredded

1 cup tomatoes, diced

1 cup spinach

salt and pepper, to taste

Directions

In a bowl, beat 8 eggs with salt and pepper. Arrange mozzarella in the center of tortillas.

Lightly grease pan. Pour eggs onto skillet. Scramble until cooked but not dry. Spoon eggs onto mozzarella.

Divide tomatoes and spinach onto wraps. Tightly roll.

Place wraps in the skillet over low heat until the cheese is melted.

92 one-pan kitchen

Chicken Quesadillas

Servings: 6   **Time:** 20 minutes

Ingredients

8 tortillas (recipe on page 228)

2 cups Monterey Jack cheese

1 can diced green chilies

1 cup roasted red peppers, thinly sliced

1 lb chicken, cooked and shredded

2 tbsp olive oil, divided

1 cup salsa

sour cream, to garnish

Directions

In the skillet, heat 1 tablespoon of olive oil on medium heat. Place two tortillas in skillet and top each with ¼ cup shredded cheese, ¼ of the chicken, ¼ of the roasted red peppers, and ¼ of the green chilies. Top with another ¼ cup of cheese and a tortilla.

Cook for 2-5 minutes or until cheese is melted and tortilla is crisp. Flip the tortillas and cook on the other side. Repeat with remaining tortillas. Slice each quesadilla and serve with salsa and sour cream.

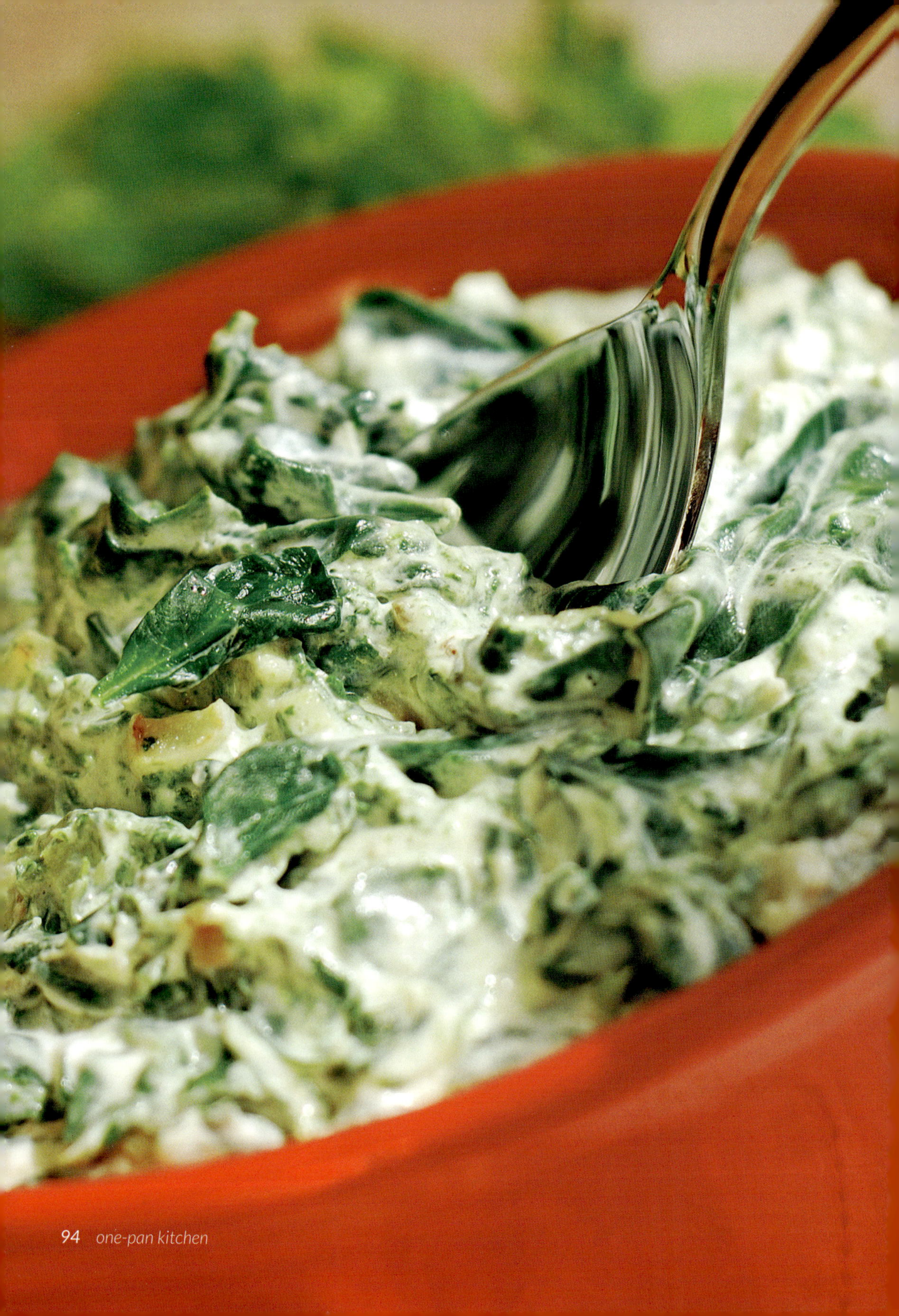

Spinach and Artichoke Dip

Servings: 8   **Time:** 15 minutes

Ingredients

1 cup frozen spinach

1 (14 oz) can artichoke hearts, drained and chopped

8 oz cream cheese

¼ cup sour cream

¼ cup mayonnaise

¼ cup Parmesan cheese

¼ cup mozzarella cheese, grated

¼ tsp salt

½ tsp onion powder

Directions

Boil water in the skillet on high. Add the frozen spinach and cook for 3 minutes. Drain and squeeze spinach dry.

Add the remaining ingredients as well as the spinach to the skillet and cook over low heat until everything is hot and melted.

Serve with pita chips.

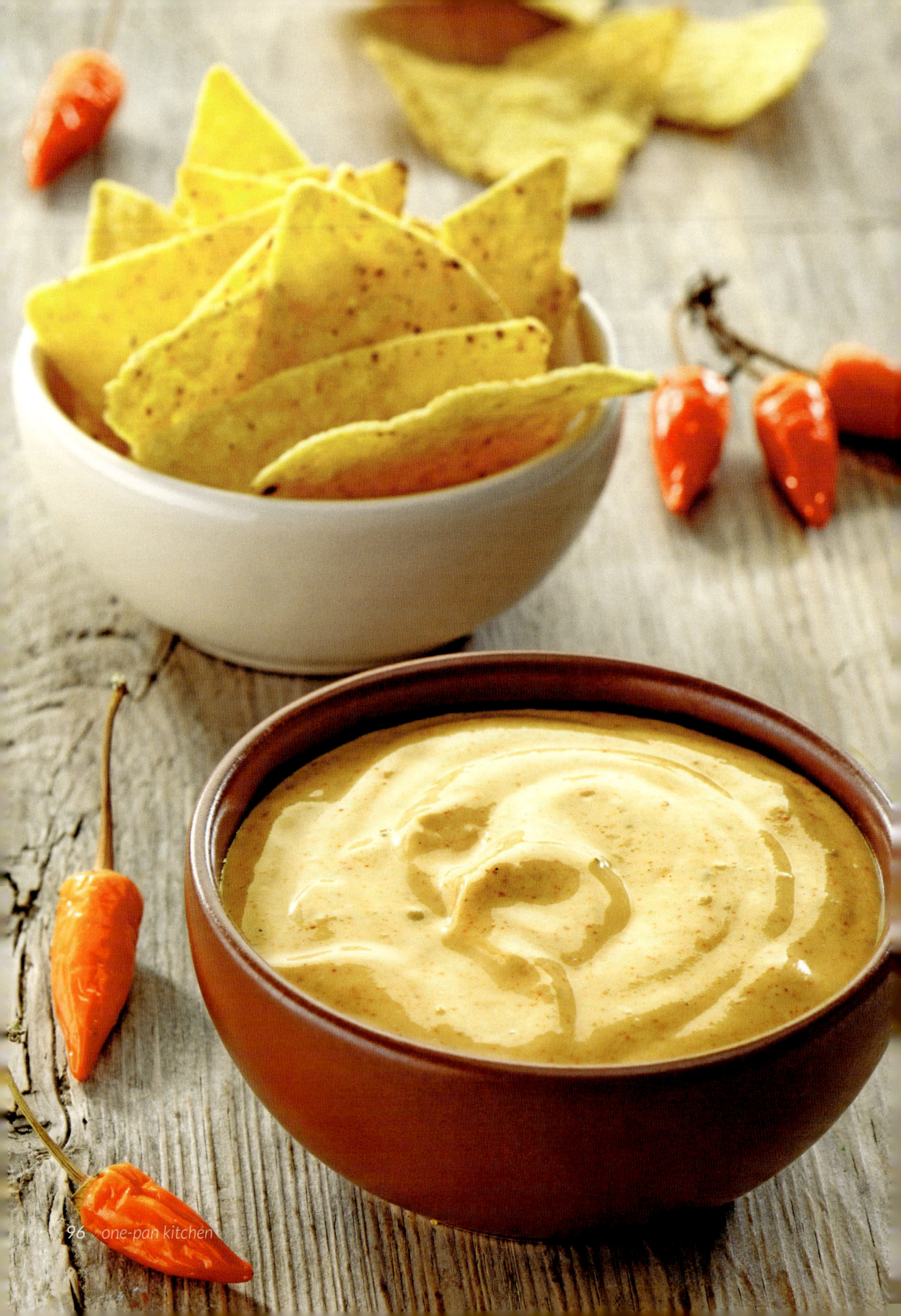

Queso Dip

Servings: 8   **Time:** 15 minutes

Ingredients

2 tbsp butter

2 tbsp flour

1 cup sour cream

1 cup cheddar cheese, grated

3 tbsp salsa

Directions

Melt butter in the skillet. Add the flour and mix well to create a roux. Cook the flour in the butter until the roux starts to emit a nutty aroma.

Add the sour cream and cook until it boils.

Add the cheese and salsa and cook until cheese is melted and the mixture has thickened.

Serve with tortilla chips.

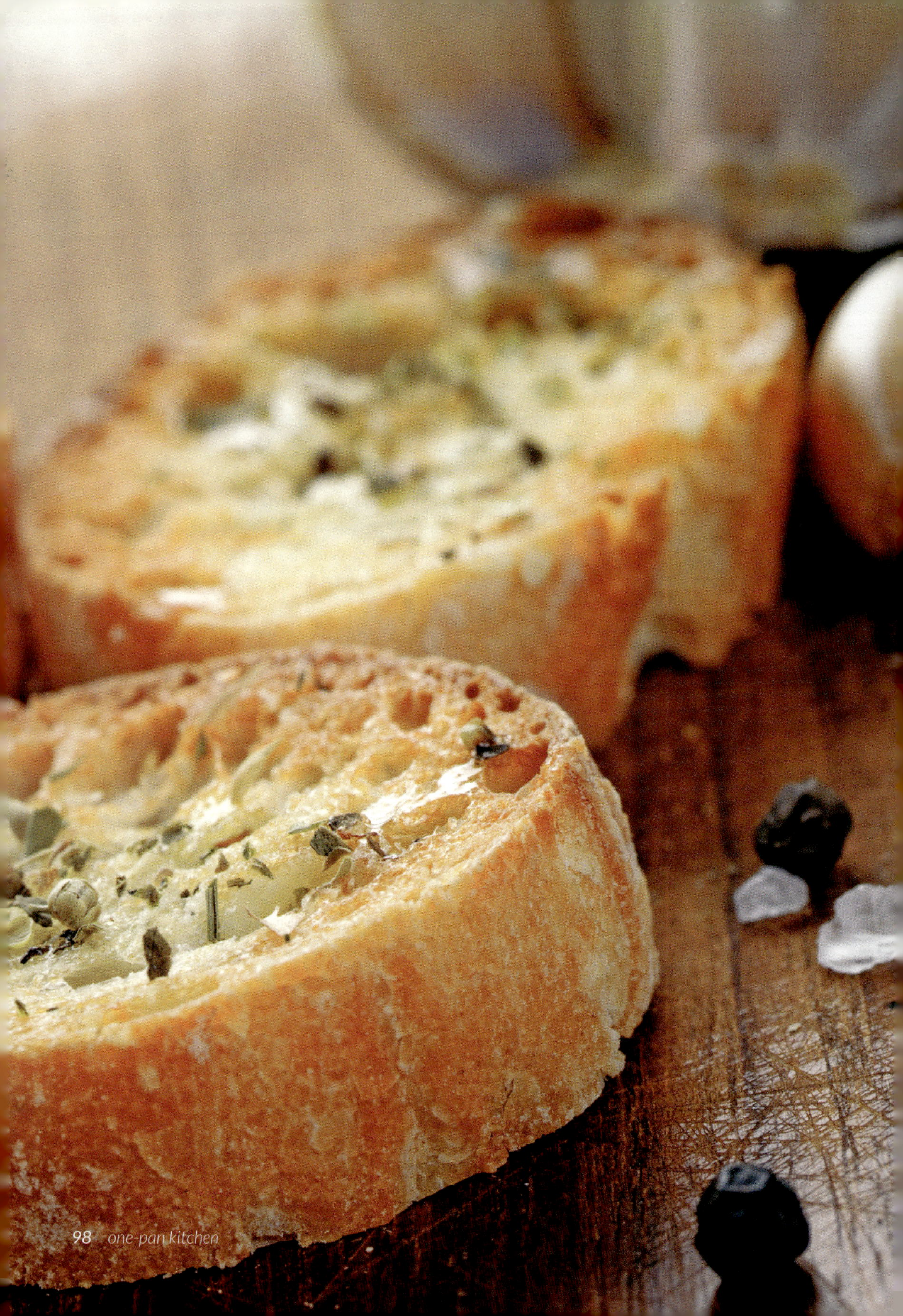

Garlic Crostini

Servings: 8-10   **Time:** 15 minutes

Ingredients

1 baguette, thinly sliced on a diagonal

¼ cup olive oil

4 gloves garlic, pressed

Italian seasoning, to taste

salt and black pepper, to taste

Directions

Drizzle olive oil over baguette slices and top with pressed garlic. Sprinkle with Italian seasoning, salt, and pepper. Cover the bottom of the skillet with the baguette slices and turn the skillet to medium heat.

Flip the bread slices every few minutes to ensure they are evenly toasted. Cook until golden brown and crunchy.

New England Clam Chowder   pg 116-117

Soups & Stews

102-103	Hearty Beef Stew
104-105	Classic Tomato Soup
106-107	Chickpea Stew
108-109	Garden Vegetable Soup
110-111	Lasagna Soup
112-113	Traditional Shepherd's Pie
114	Chicken Shepherd's Pie
115	Eggplant Curry
116-117	New England Clam Chowder
118-119	Cornbread Chili
120-121	Veggie Chili
122-123	Turkey and Black Bean Chili
124-125	Green Chili with Pork
126-127	White Chili

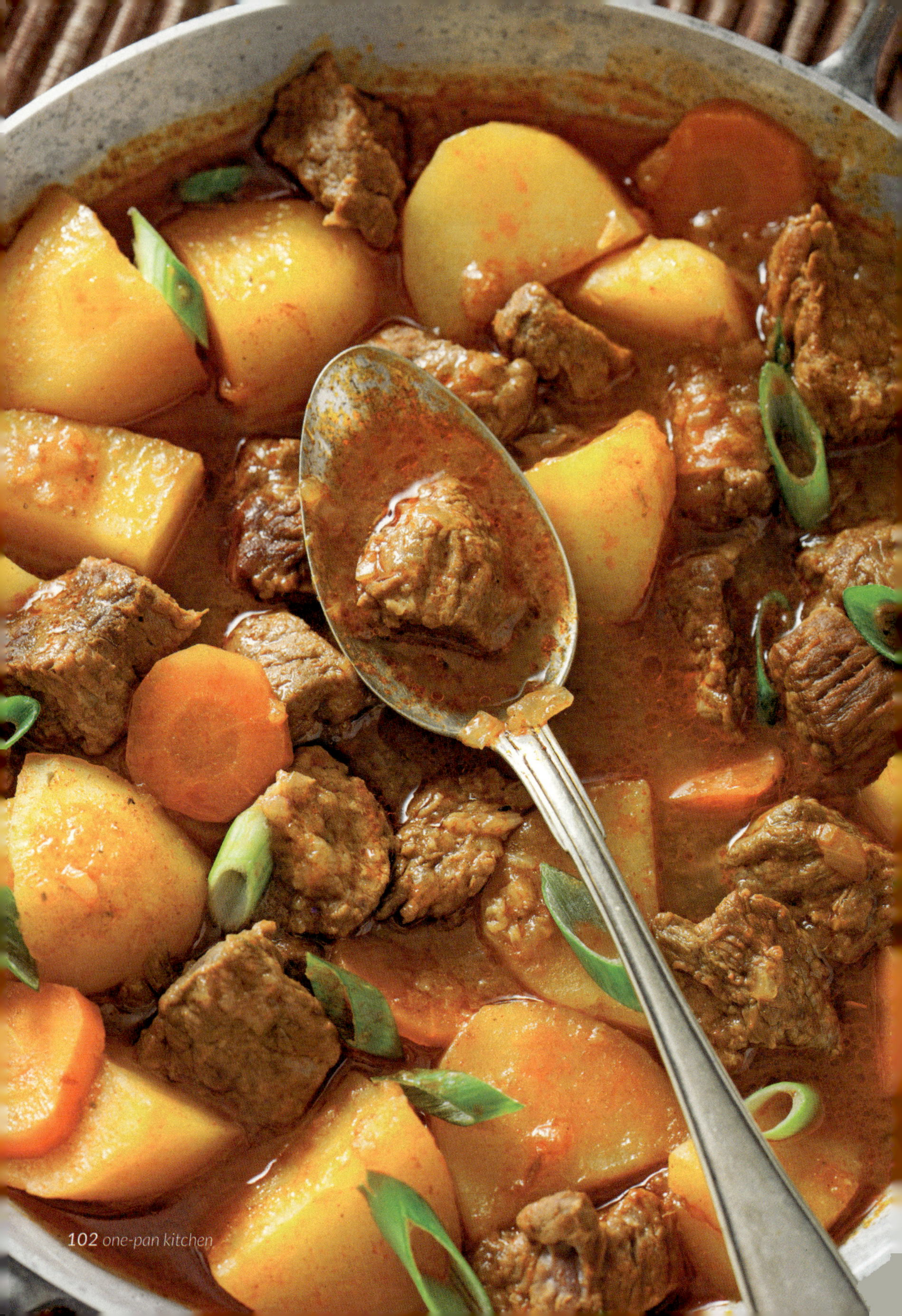

Hearty Beef Stew

Servings: 12-18 **Time:** 3 hours

Ingredients

3 lbs boneless chuck roast, cut into 1½" pieces

2 tbsp olive oil

1 yellow onion, diced

3 cloves garlic, minced

2 tbsp balsamic vinegar

2 tbsp tomato paste

2 cups red wine

4 cups beef broth

¼ cup flour

6 sprigs fresh thyme

4 large carrots, peeled and cut into 1" chunks

1 lb small white potatoes, halved

1 bag frozen pearl onions

1 bag frozen green peas

2 tsp salt

1 tsp freshly ground black pepper

thinly sliced green onions, to garnish (optional)

Directions

Heat skillet to medium. Add oil to skillet. Once the pan is hot, add beef in a single layer. Sprinkle with salt and pepper.

Cook beef until browned on all sides, about 5 minutes. Then, add yellow onion and garlic. Cook 2 minutes more, stirring often.

Turn heat to low and add balsamic vinegar, tomato paste, and flour. Stir until meat is coated. Stir in wine, beef broth, and thyme. Cover and let cook about 1½ hours.

Add carrots, potatoes, and pearl onions. Continue cooking another hour. Add peas and cook for 5 more minutes. Adjust seasonings to taste, garnish with green onions, and serve.

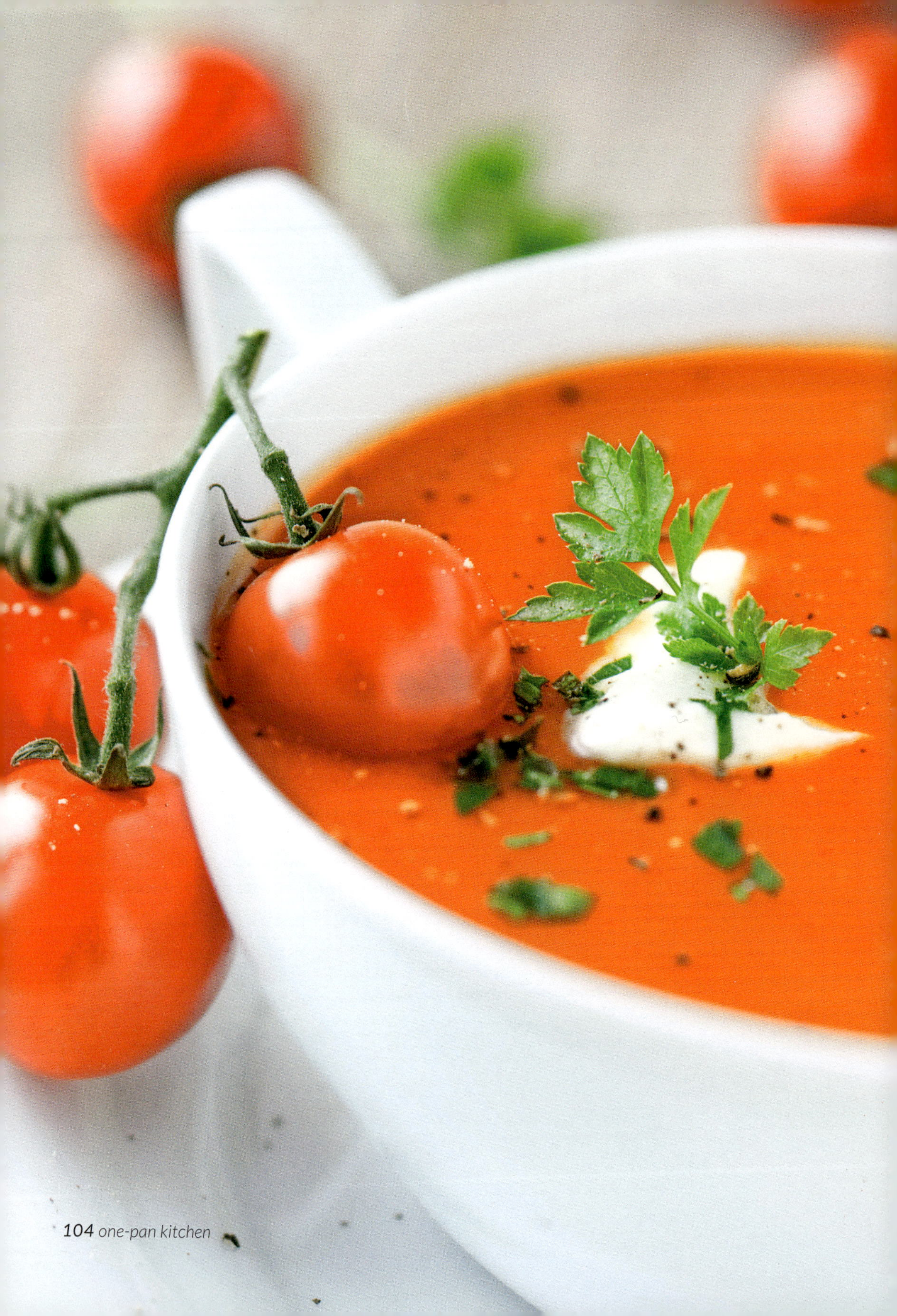

Classic Tomato Soup

Servings: 8–12   **Time:** 30 minutes

Ingredients

1 stick (½ cup) unsalted butter or olive oil

3 medium yellow onions, thinly sliced

2 tsp salt

2 tbsp curry powder

2 tsp ground coriander

2 tsp ground cumin

1 tsp chili flakes

3 (28 oz) cans whole tomatoes (preferably fire-roasted)

dollop of cream or coconut milk

6 cups water

Directions

Set the skillet to medium heat and melt the butter. Add the onions and salt. Cook the onions for 10 minutes or until soft, stirring occasionally.

Add curry powder, coriander, cumin, and chili flakes. Cook until the spices are fragrant (about 30 seconds).

Mix in tomatoes, their juices, and water. Simmer for 15 minutes.

Purée with a hand blender until smooth.

For a thinner soup, add more water. For a creamier texture, pour in a little cream or coconut milk.

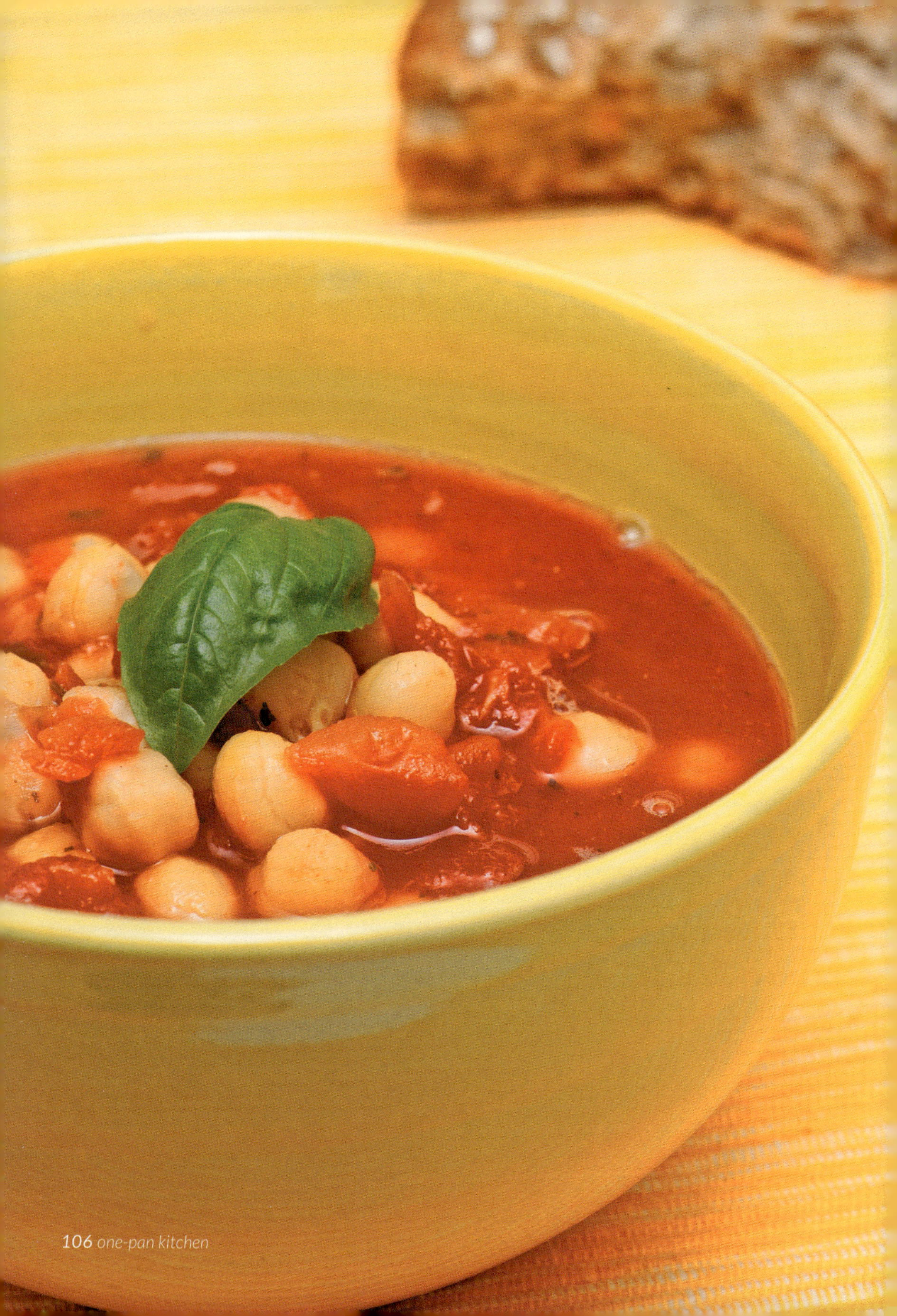

Chickpea Stew

Servings: 8–12   **Time:** 1 hour

Ingredients

8 boneless chicken thighs

¼ cup olive oil, divided

2 medium onions, chopped

2 green bell peppers, chopped

2 garlic cloves, chopped

dash of red pepper flakes

2 tsp cumin

2 (15 oz) cans diced tomatoes, undrained

2 (15 oz) cans chickpeas, undrained

1 cup dried cranberries

dollop of plain yogurt (optional)

Directions

In the skillet, sauté the onions and bell peppers in 1 tablespoon of oil until translucent.

Add the garlic, pepper flakes, and cumin. Stir for about 1 minute before removing from skillet and setting aside.

Add the remaining 3 tablespoons of oil to the skillet. Add the chicken and cook on medium heat until it starts to brown. Flip and brown the other side. Place chicken on the plate with the vegetables.

Deglaze the skillet by pouring in some of the juice from the canned tomatoes.

Once the solids in the pan have dissolved, add the chicken, vegetables, tomatoes, chickpeas, and cranberries.

Cover and let simmer on low for about 30 minutes or until the chicken is cooked through.

108 *one-pan kitchen*

Garden Vegetable Soup

Servings: 12-18   **Time:** 45-60 minutes

Ingredients

2-3 quarts low-sodium chicken broth

4 tbsp olive oil

2 medium onions, diced

4 medium carrots, peeled and diced

6 medium garlic cloves, finely chopped

2 cups fresh green beans, diced

1 cup fresh corn kernels

1 cup chickpeas

1 cup squash, diced

1 lime, freshly squeezed

salt and pepper, to taste

Directions

Heat olive oil in skillet over medium heat. Add the onions and cook until slightly brown.

Add the carrots, green beans, squash, and garlic to the pan. Cook for about 4-5 minutes. Pour in the chicken broth and increase heat to high.

Let the soup come to a boil. Then reduce to a simmer. Add the corn and chickpeas.

Reduce the heat to low. Cover and cook until the vegetables are fork tender (about 15-30 minutes).

Remove from heat and add lime juice. Season with salt and pepper.

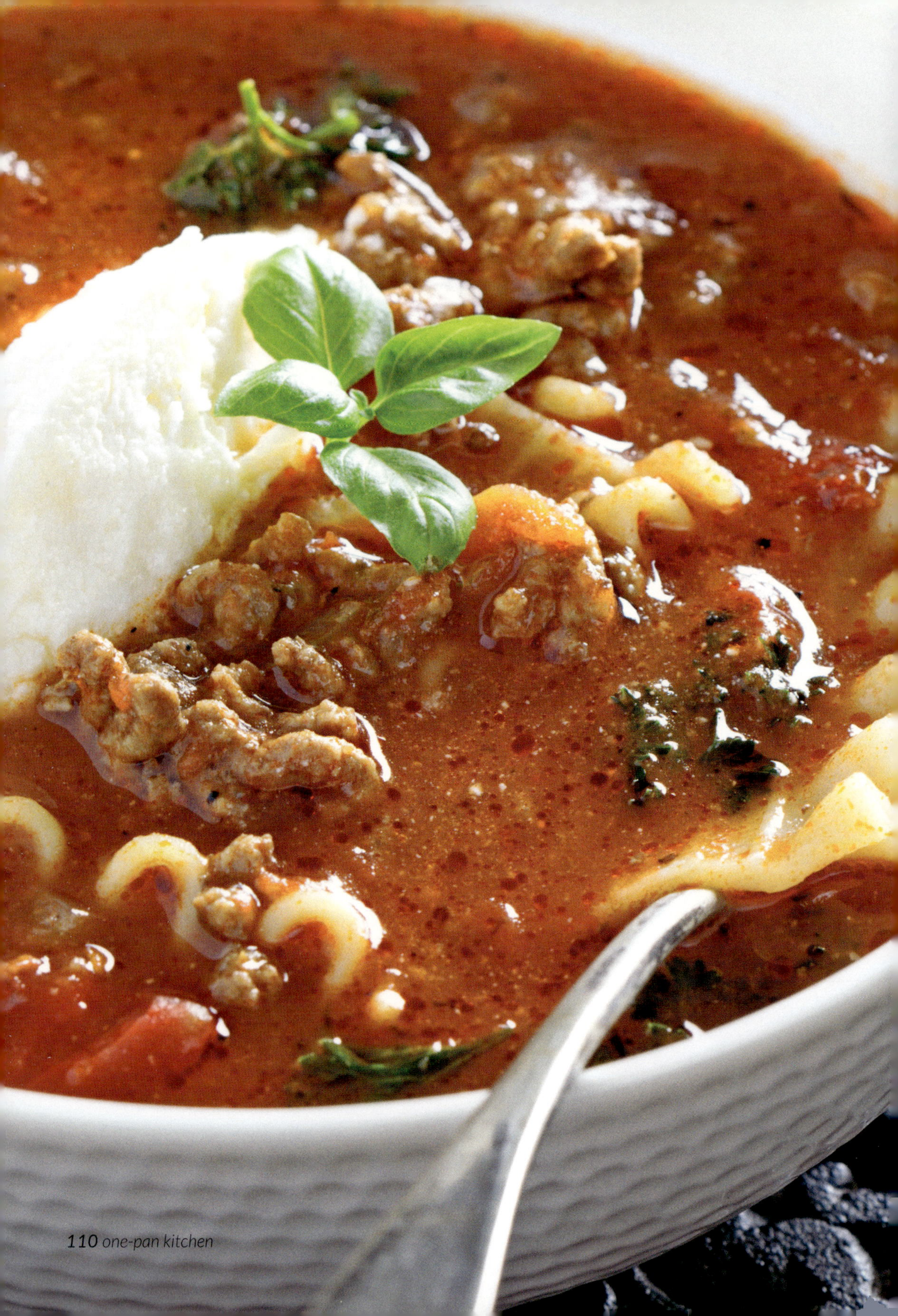

Lasagna Soup

Servings: 4-6   **Time:** 45-60 minutes

Ingredients

Soup:

1 lb ground beef

1 lb ground sausage

2 yellow onions, chopped

2 cloves garlic, minced

2 tsp dried oregano

½ tsp red pepper flakes

1 tsp salt

2 (14.5 oz) cans diced tomatoes

4 cups chicken broth

¼ cup fresh basil leaves, chopped

½ lb lasagna noodles, broken into smaller squares

Topping:

1 cup ricotta cheese

½ cup grated Parmesan cheese

¼ tsp salt

fresh basil

Directions

In the skillet, brown the beef and sausage with the onions. Drain any excess grease and add the minced garlic, oregano, salt, and red pepper flakes. Cook for 2 minutes. Add the canned tomatoes and chicken broth. Simmer for 20 minutes.

Bring the soup to a boil. Then, reduce the heat and simmer for 20-30 minutes. Add the fresh basil and the lasagna noodles. Cook for 10 minutes at a low simmer.

Meanwhile, in a small bowl, mix the ricotta cheese, Parmesan cheese, and salt together. Serve soup with a dollop of the ricotta cheese topping and fresh basil.

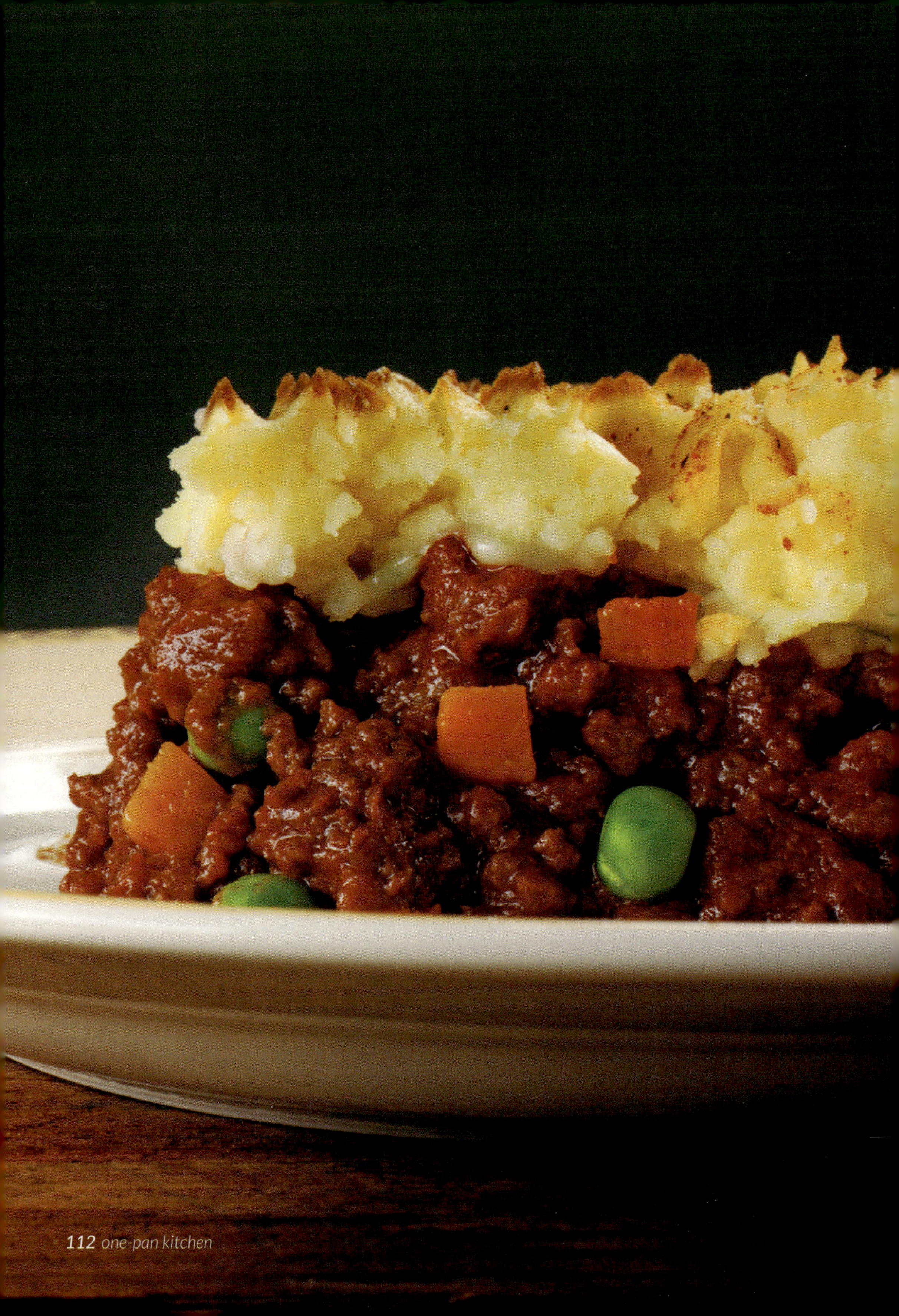

Traditional Shepherd's Pie

Servings: 6-8 **Time:** 1 hour

Ingredients

5 potatoes, peeled and chopped (2 lbs)

¼ cup sour cream

2 tbsp olive oil

1 onion, chopped

2 carrots, chopped

2 lbs ground beef

1 tsp salt

2 tbsp butter

2 tbsp all-purpose flour

2 tbsp ketchup

1 cup chicken broth

1 (14.5 oz) can diced tomatoes

½ cup peas

Directions

In the skillet, boil water. Add potatoes and cook until soft. Drain potatoes and mash with sour cream. Salt to taste.

Sauté the onion and ground beef for about 5 minutes in the olive oil. Add the carrots and cook for another 5 minutes.

Mix in the butter and flour. Cook until fragrant. Slowly pour in the chicken stock and mix well. Add in the ketchup, diced tomatoes, corn, and peas.

Cook for about 10 minutes or until the sauce thickens. Season with salt and pepper. Top with mashed potatoes. Cover and cook for 10 minutes.

Chicken Shepherd's Pie

Servings: 6–8   **Time:** 1 hour

Ingredients

4 chicken breasts, diced

5 potatoes, peeled and chopped (2 lbs)

1 tbsp olive oil

2 onions, chopped

2 carrots, peeled and chopped

½ cup corn

½ cup peas

4 tbsp butter

4 tbsp flour

4 cups chicken stock

salt and pepper, to taste

¼ cup sour cream

Directions

Boil water over high heat in the skillet. Add potatoes and cook until soft. Drain potatoes and mash with sour cream and salt.

Sauté the onions for about 5 minutes over medium heat. Add the chicken to pan and brown.

Add the butter and flour. Mix until fragrant. Slowly pour in the chicken stock and mix well. Add in the carrots, corn, and peas. Cook for about 10 minutes or until the sauce thickens and the chicken is cooked through.

Season with salt and pepper. Top with mashed potatoes. Cover and cook an additional 10 minutes.

Eggplant Curry

Servings: 4-6   **Time:** 1 hour

Ingredients

1 large eggplant, diced

¼ cup butter

1 large yellow onion, diced

1 red bell pepper, sliced

1 serrano pepper, diced

1½ tbsp curry powder

1 tbsp apricot jam

1 tbsp soy sauce

1 (14 oz) can diced tomatoes

1 (14 oz) can chickpeas, drained

¾ cup full fat coconut milk

4 cups vegetable broth

1 tsp salt

½ tsp pepper

limes and cilantro, to garnish

Directions

Melt the butter in the skillet over medium heat. Add the onion, serrano pepper, red bell pepper, and curry powder. Sauté until the onion is translucent. Add eggplant, jam, soy sauce, diced tomatoes, and chickpeas and cook for 5 minutes.

Stir in the coconut milk, vegetable broth, salt, and pepper. Reduce the heat to low and simmer for about 30 minutes. Use an immersion blender to blend the soup to your desired consistency. Garnish with limes and fresh cilantro.

116 one-pan kitchen

New England Clam Chowder

Servings: 4-6 **Time:** 20 minutes

Ingredients

3 medium red potatoes, chopped

2 stalks celery, chopped

1 medium onion, diced

1 cup frozen corn

3 (6.5 oz) cans chopped clams

4 tbsp butter

4 tbsp flour

1 cup half & half

1 cup milk

2 tbsp vinegar

oyster crackers, to garnish

Directions

Add red potatoes, celery, onion, and frozen corn to skillet over medium heat. Add butter and sauté for 5 minutes.

Mix in flour and stir until fragrant. Add the juice from the canned clams and simmer for 2 minutes. Then, pour in milk and half & half.

Simmer for 15 minutes. Five minutes before serving, add the canned clams and vinegar. Cook 2 minutes and serve with oyster crackers.

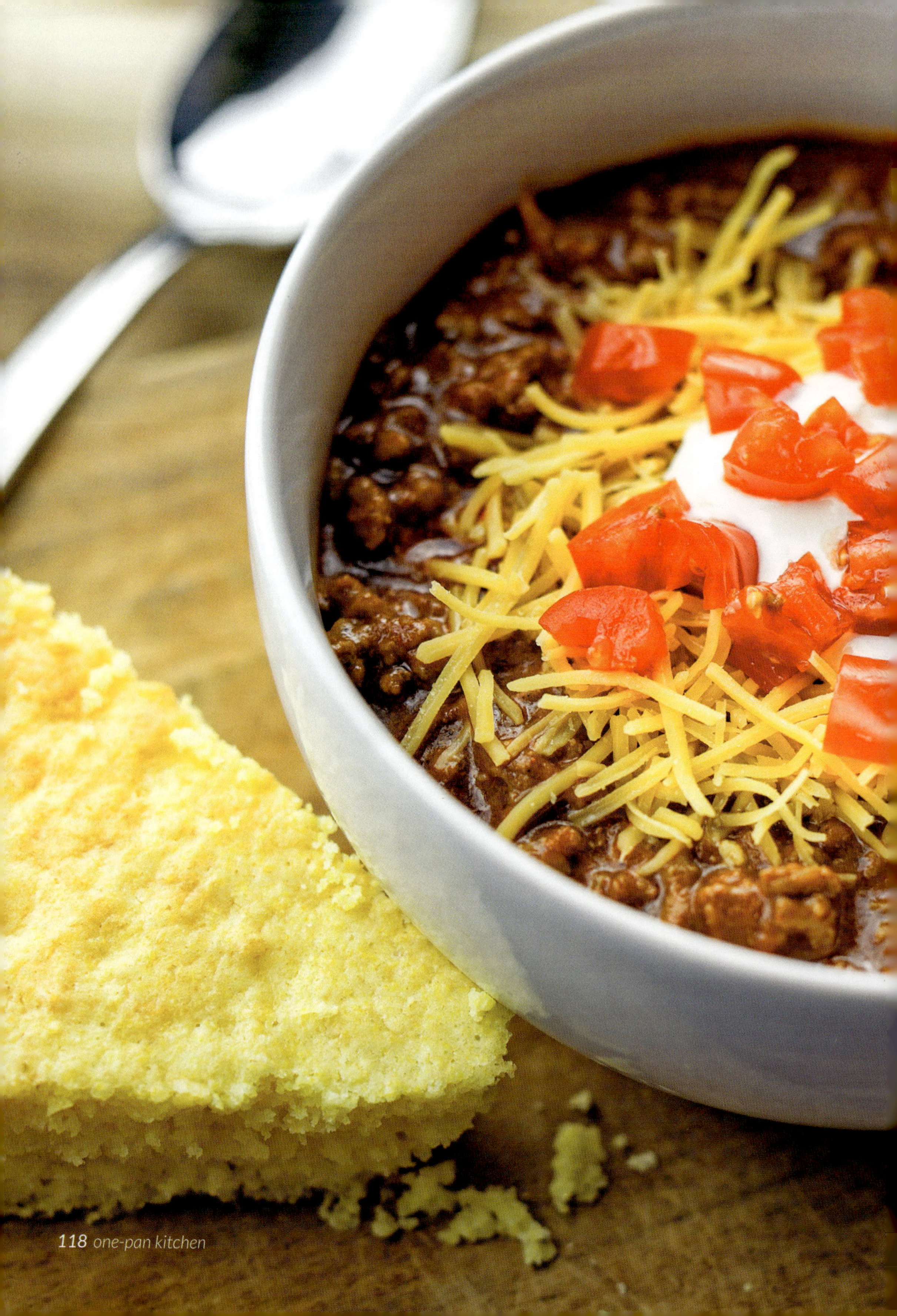

Cornbread Chili

Servings: 6   **Time:** 45 minutes

Ingredients

Chili:
2 tbsp olive oil
1 lb ground beef
1 yellow onion, chopped
1 bell pepper, chopped
2 cloves garlic, minced
½ tsp oregano
1 tsp cumin
1 tsp chili powder
1 tsp onion powder
1 tsp salt
¼ tsp ground black pepper
1 (8 oz) can tomato sauce
2 (14.5 oz) cans diced tomatoes
1 can red kidney beans
1 small can chopped black olives, drained

Cornbread and Topping:
1 cup flour
¾ cup cornmeal
¼ tsp baking soda
½ tsp baking powder
¼ cup vegetable oil
1 egg
1 (8 oz) can creamed corn
½ cup buttermilk
1 cup cheddar cheese, shredded

Directions

In the skillet, heat the oil on medium heat and add the ground beef, yellow onion, and bell pepper. Sauté for 5 minutes. Then, add the garlic and spices and cook for another 2 minutes. Stir in the tomato sauce, canned tomatoes, beans, and olives. Reduce heat to low and cover.

While the chili simmers, make the cornbread topping. In a medium bowl, mix the dry ingredients. Then, add the oil, egg, creamed corn, and buttermilk. Mix until combined.

Uncover the chili, top with cheese, and dot with the cornbread mixture. Turn the skillet to medium low and cover to bake for 20-30 minutes or until the cornbread is cooked through.

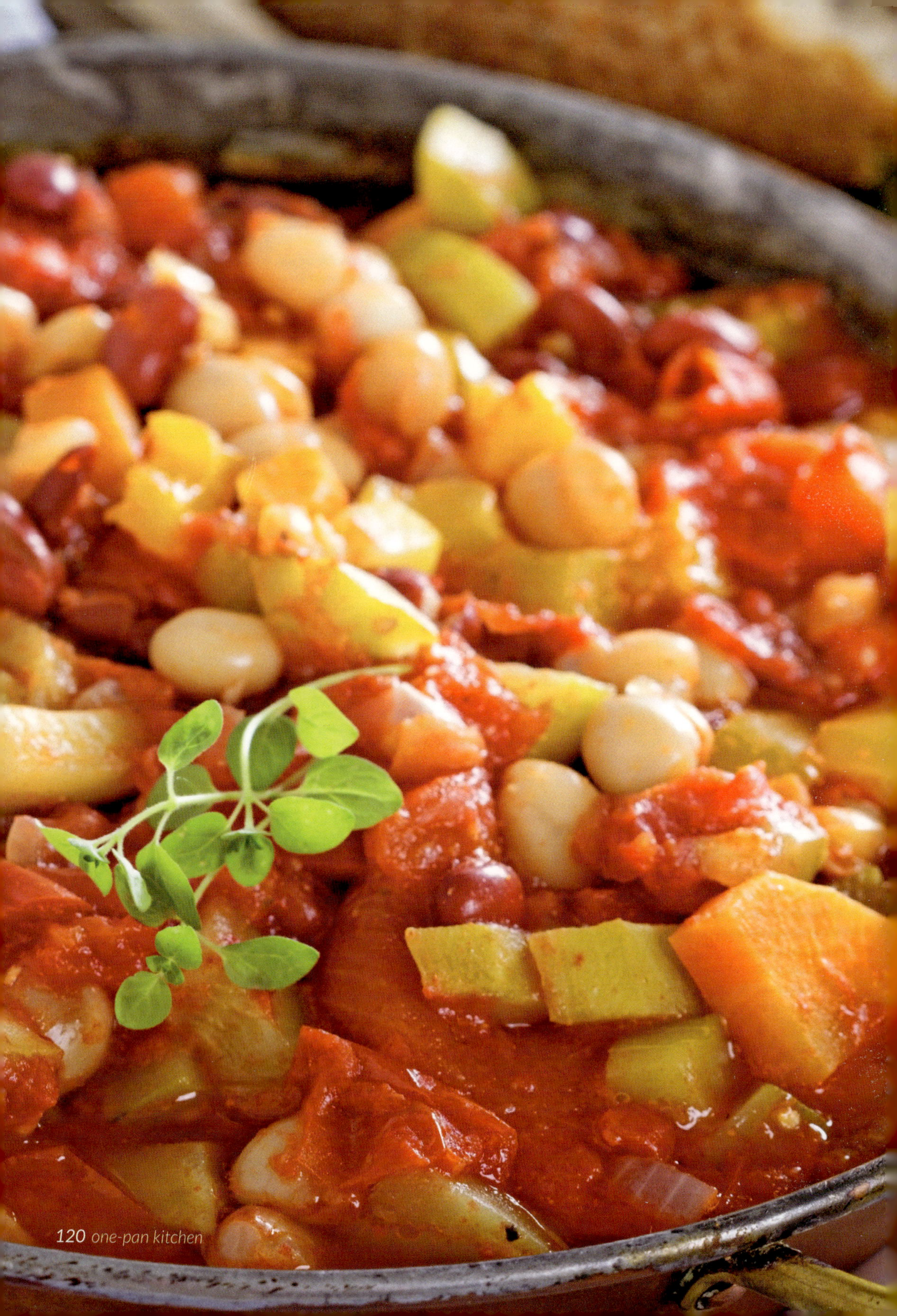

Veggie Chili

Servings: 6   **Time:** 45 minutes

Ingredients

1 lb sweet potatoes, cubed

2 tbsp olive oil

1 yellow onion, chopped

1 bell pepper, chopped

4 stalks celery, diced

4 medium carrots, peeled and sliced

3 cloves garlic, minced

1 tsp oregano

1 tsp cumin

1 tsp chili powder

1 tsp smoked paprika

1 tsp onion powder

1 tsp salt

¼ tsp ground black pepper

2 (14.5 oz) cans diced tomatoes

1 can white beans

1 can red beans

Directions

Heat the oil in the skillet on medium and add the yellow onion, cubed sweet potato, celery, carrots, and bell pepper. Sauté for 10 minutes. Then, add the garlic and spices and cook for another 2 minutes.

Stir in the canned tomatoes and beans. Cover and simmer for 30 minutes.

122 one-pan kitchen

Turkey and Black Bean Chili

Servings: 6   **Time:** 45 minutes

Ingredients

1 lb ground turkey

2 tbsp olive oil

1 yellow onion, chopped

1 yellow bell pepper, chopped

2 cloves garlic, minced

1 tsp cumin

1 tsp chili powder

1 tsp onion powder

1 tsp salt

¼ tsp ground black pepper

2 (14.5 oz) cans diced tomatoes

1 can black beans

Directions

Heat the oil in the skillet over medium heat and add the ground turkey, yellow onion, and bell pepper.

Sauté for 10 minutes. Add in the garlic and spices and cook for another 2 minutes.

Stir in the canned tomatoes and black beans.

Cover and simmer for 30 minutes.

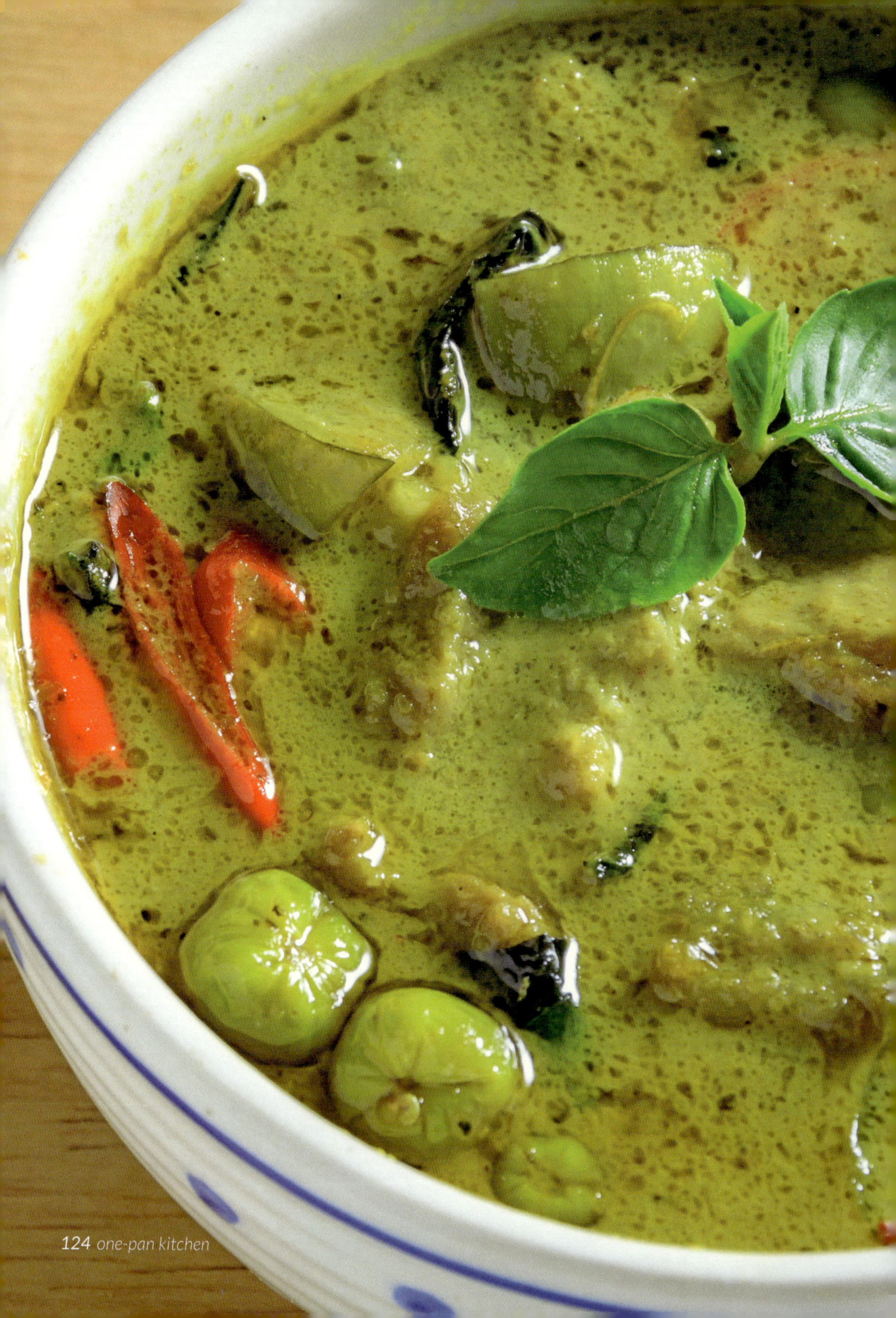

Green Chili with Pork

Servings: 4   **Time:** 1 hour

Ingredients

1½ lbs pork shoulder, cubed

4 Anaheim chiles

1 medium yellow onion, diced

½ cup chopped cilantro

6 fresh tomatillos, chopped

4 cloves garlic, minced

2 tbsp flour

4 cups chicken stock

4 tbsp oil, divided

1 tsp cumin

salt and black pepper, to taste

limes and sour cream, to garnish

Directions

Coat the Anaheim chiles in oil and place in the skillet on medium heat. Cook with the lid on, turning occasionally, for 15 minutes. Remove chiles and let cool. Then, deseed and chop the chiles and set aside.

Add the remaining oil to the skillet and sauté the onion, pork, and tomatillos until the pork is brown and the onion is translucent. Season with salt and pepper.

Add the chiles, cumin, garlic, cilantro, and flour. Cook for another 2 minutes. Pour in the chicken stock and simmer for 30 minutes with the lid on. Simmer uncovered for another 15 minutes. Serve with limes and sour cream.

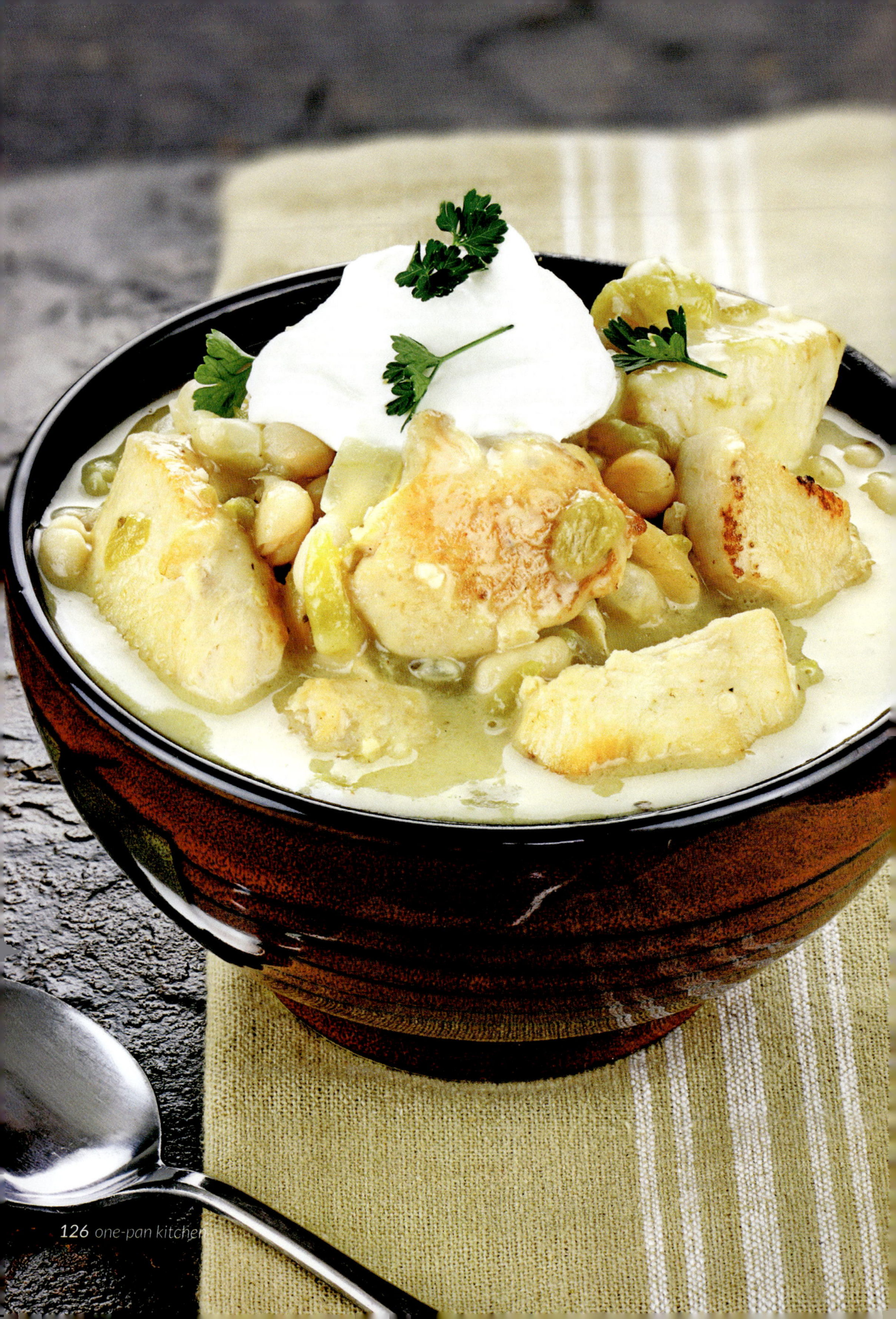

White Chili

Servings: 6   **Time:** 1 hour

Ingredients

1 lb boneless, skinless chicken breasts

1 medium onion, chopped

2 garlic cloves, chopped

1 tbsp canola oil

2 (15.5 oz) cans great northern beans, rinsed and drained

1 (14.5 oz) can chicken broth

1 (4 oz) can diced green chiles

1 tsp ground cumin

1 tsp dried oregano

¼ tsp cayenne pepper

1 cup sour cream

1-2 cups Monterey Jack cheese, shredded

salt and pepper, to taste

Directions

Over medium heat, sauté the chicken and onion in the oil until the chicken is no longer pink and the onion is translucent.

Add the garlic, cumin, oregano, and cayenne pepper. Stir for another minute. Add the broth and deglaze the pan.

Add the beans and chiles and bring to a boil. Reduce the heat to low; simmer, uncovered, for about 30 minutes.

Turn off the heat, remove the chicken, and cut into bite-size pieces. Return chicken to the chili and stir in the sour cream. Slowly add in the shredded cheese in small handfuls until the cheese is incorporated.

Serve with tomatoes, additional cheese, cilantro, and additional sour cream.

Caitlin Wise

"I ask for white chili for my birthday dinner every year. Mind you, my birthday is in the summer so it must be amazingly good in order for me to want chili on a hot day. It is creamy, tangy, has heat, and is amazingly comforting."

Rosemary Steak   pg 158-159

Entrées

130-131	Mussels Mariniere	164-165	Classic Tomato Sauce
132-133	Paella	166-167	Italian Style Meatballs
134-135	Ginger Garlic Shrimp Stir-Fry	168-169	Classic Lasagna
136-137	Chipotle Shrimp Tacos	170-171	Firehouse Chili
138-139	Lemon Pepper Cod	172-173	Korean Bbq Beef
140-141	Pan Fried Tilapia	174-175	Pepper Beef
142-143	Crispy Skin Salmon	176-177	Pear & Ginger Pork
144-145	Buttermilk Fried Chicken	178-179	Pork Chops With Apple Gravy
146-147	Thai Peanut Curry	180-181	Hearty Cornbread Dressing
148-149	Red Curry	182-183	Carnitas Pizza
150-151	Chicken Parmigiana	184-185	Eggplant Parmigiana
152-153	Chicken Pizzaiola	186-187	Korean Stir-Fried Noodles (Japcchae)
154-155	Lemon Chicken with Spinach & Mushrooms	188-189	Zucchini Burger
156-157	Apricot Chicken with Bell Peppers	190-191	Gourmet Grilled Cheese
158-159	Rosemary Steak	192-193	Butternut Squash & Kale Linguine
160-161	Classic Cheese Burger		
162-163	Mumma Bumma's Meatballs		

130 one-pan kitchen

Mussels Mariniere

Servings: 4-6   **Time:** 30 minutes

Ingredients

5 lbs mussels, cleaned

3 small shallots, minced

1 medium yellow onion, diced

2 cloves of garlic, minced

1 bottle dry white wine

1 tbsp olive oil

½ cup (1 stick) butter, divided

2 bay leaves

2 sprigs fresh thyme

¼ cup fresh parsley, chopped

freshly ground black pepper, to taste

Directions

In a skillet over medium heat, add olive oil and 2 tablespoons butter. Mix in the diced onion, shallots, and garlic.

Once the onions soften and become fragrant, add the bay leaves and thyme and stir the mixture for 30 seconds. Add the white wine and bring to a boil. Set the heat to low and simmer for 2-3 minutes.

Add the mussels and cover with the lid. Cook for 3-4 minutes until the mussels open. Discard any mussels that do not open. Using a slotted spoon, transfer the mussels to a bowl, leaving the sauce in the pan. Add the remaining butter, parsley, and black pepper to the pan. Stir until the butter melts and then turn off the heat. Add the mussels back to the pan and coat with the sauce.

Serve with slices of toasted french bread.

132 one-pan kitchen

Paella

Servings: 6-8   **Time:** 30 minutes

Ingredients

2 lbs assorted raw fresh seafood (shrimp, mussels, clams)

2 tbsp olive oil

3 cloves garlic, crushed

1 green pepper, diced

1 onion, diced

1 tsp crushed red pepper flakes

1 tsp salt

2 cups valencia white rice, uncooked

1 pinch saffron threads

1 bay leaf

½ bunch parsley, chopped

4 cups chicken stock

2 lemons, juiced and zested

peas and sliced pimiento, to garnish (optional)

Directions

Heat 2 tablespoons olive oil in skillet on medium heat. Add onion, green pepper, garlic, red pepper flakes, salt, and rice. Cook for about 3 minutes until vegetables are tender. Stir in saffron threads, bay leaf, parsley, chicken stock, lemon juice, and zest.

Bring to a boil, cover, and reduce heat to low. Simmer for 15 minutes. Uncover, add shrimp, mussels, and clams on top (do not stir). Cover and let cook another 5-7 minutes until seafood is done. Garnish with peas and sliced pimiento.

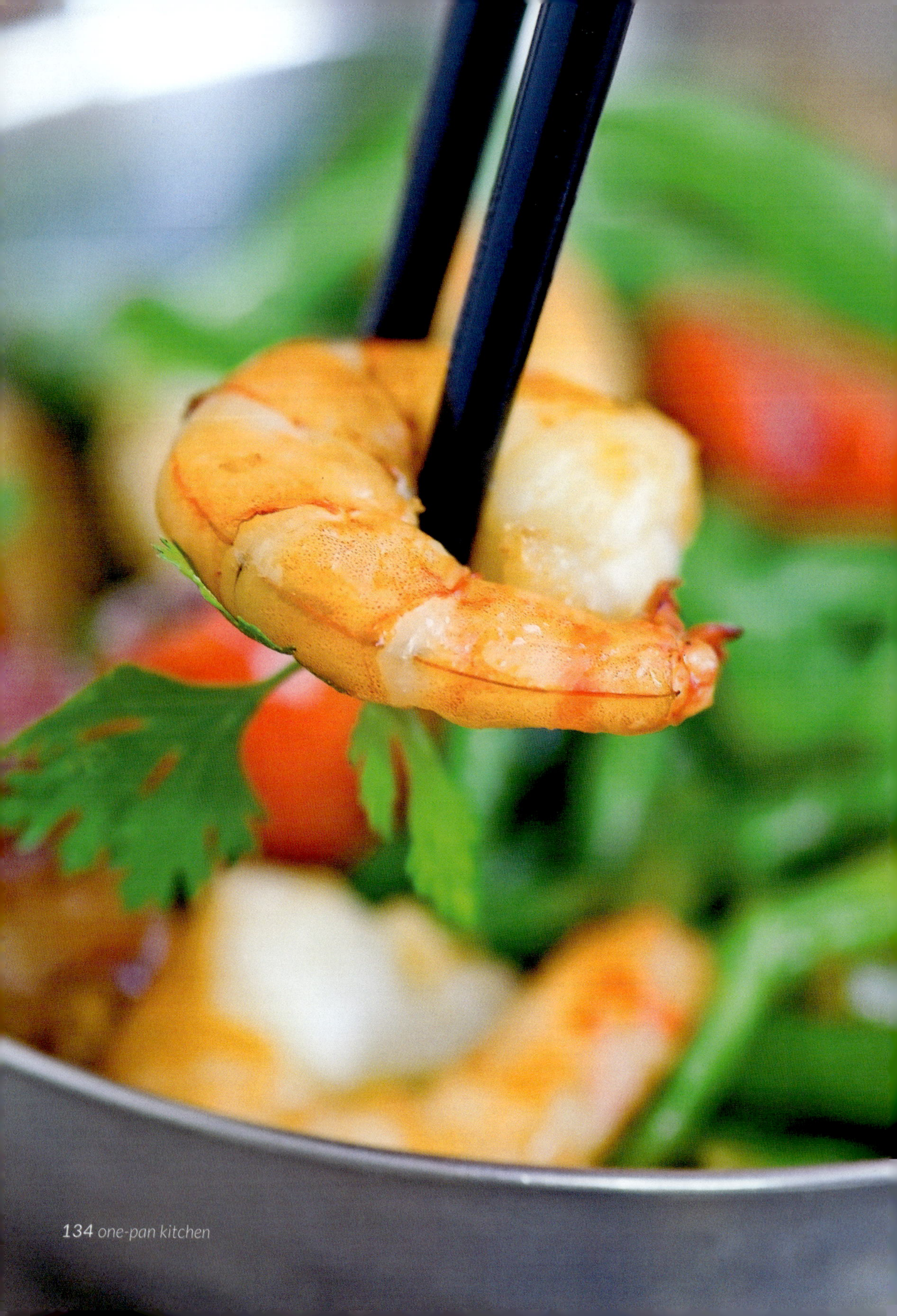

Ginger Garlic Shrimp Stir-Fry

Servings: 4-6 **Time:** 15 minutes

Ingredients

1½ lbs raw medium shrimp, peeled and cleaned

2 tbsp soy sauce

¼ cup oyster sauce

handful cilantro, chopped

3 tbsp sesame oil

4 cloves garlic, minced

2 tbsp ginger, minced

1 red bell pepper, sliced

2 green onions, chopped

1 cup sugar snap peas

1 cup broccoli, chopped

1 cup mushrooms, sliced

black pepper, to taste

sesame seeds, to garnish

Directions

In a bowl, combine soy sauce, oyster sauce, and cilantro. Set aside.

In skillet, heat sesame oil, ginger, and garlic over medium heat. Add shrimp and cook until it starts to turn pink (about 2 minutes per side). When shrimp is almost cooked through, remove with slotted silicone spoon and set aside.

Add bell pepper, green onion, snap peas, broccoli, and mushrooms and sauté over medium heat. Once vegetables are tender, return shrimp to the skillet.

Pour soy sauce mixture over the shrimp and vegetables and stir.

Season with pepper and garnish with sesame seeds.

136 one-pan kitchen

Chipotle Shrimp Tacos

Servings: 4   **Time:** 15 minutes

Ingredients

1½ lbs cooked large shrimp, peeled and cut in half

1½ tbsp olive oil

1½ cup red onion, diced

3 tsp cajun seasoning

8 corn tortillas

3 limes, juiced

2 cups cheese, shredded

1 cup green onion, diced

3 pitted avocados, cut into pieces

1 orange, cut into pieces

salt, to taste

Directions

In a bowl, combine shrimp and cajun seasoning. Season with salt. Toss until the shrimp is fully coated and then set aside.

Heat olive oil and red onions in skillet on medium heat. Stir until red onions are sizzling. Next, add the shrimp and lime juice. Cook for about 2-3 minutes or until shrimp is warm. Set aside the shrimp and wipe the skillet clean.

Warm tortillas over low heat. Top tortillas with cajun shrimp, shredded cheese, green onion, avocado, and orange slices.

Serve with your favorite sides.

138 one-pan kitchen

Lemon Pepper Cod

Servings: 6   **Time:** 15 minutes

Ingredients

6 (4 oz) cod fillets

2 lemons

salt and pepper, to taste

2 tbsp vegetable oil

drizzle of olive oil, to garnish

Directions

Season cod fillets with salt and pepper.

Lightly grease skillet with oil and set to high heat.

Place cod on skillet and squeeze one lemon over the fillets. Make sure skillet is hot before placing cod on the skillet.

When fish is halfway cooked through, flip and squeeze the remaining lemon juice over the fillets.

Serve fish with vegetables and a drizzle of olive oil.

140 one-pan kitchen

Pan Fried Tilapia

Servings: 4   **Time:** 15 minutes

Ingredients

4 tilapia fillets
½ cup Italian style breadcrumbs
2 cloves garlic, crushed
2 tbsp olive oil or grapeseed oil
1 lime
salt and pepper, to taste

Directions

Pour breadcrumbs into a bowl. Season tilapia with salt and pepper. Then, dip the tilapia fillets in the breadcrumbs so that each side is lightly coated.

In a skillet, heat the olive oil and garlic on medium to medium high heat.

Once oil is hot, place the tilapia in the pan. Flip the fillets after a few minutes.

Once cooked, squeeze a lime over the fish and serve with roasted potatoes and your favorite veggies.

142 one-pan kitchen

Crispy Skin Salmon

Servings: 4 **Time:** 15 minutes

Ingredients

4 (6 oz) salmon fillets with skin

2-3 tbsp olive oil

parsley and sesame seeds, to garnish

salt and pepper, to taste

Directions

Season salmon with salt and pepper. Heat skillet on high with olive oil.

Place salmon, skin side down, and reduce heat to medium. Cook until well-browned on the bottom.

Flip salmon fillets and cook until salmon is just barely pink in the center.

Garnish with parsley and sesame seeds.

144 *one-pan kitchen*

Buttermilk Fried Chicken

Servings: 2   **Time:** 20 minutes

Ingredients

1 lb boneless chicken tenderloins

½ cup and 3 tbsp buttermilk, divided

¾ cup all-purpose flour

1 tsp salt

½ tsp black pepper

½ tsp garlic powder

½ tsp paprika

1 tsp baking powder

8 cups vegetable oil, for cooking

Directions

Make the breading by sifting together the flour, salt, pepper, garlic powder, paprika, and baking powder in a shallow dish. Stir in 3 tbsp of buttermilk. Pour ½ cup of buttermilk in a separate shallow dish.

Dip the chicken tenders first in the buttermilk and then in the breading. Place on a baking sheet lined with aluminum foil.

Pour ¾ inch of vegetable oil into skillet and heat on high until the oil shimmers. Use silicone tongs to place chicken in the oil. Cook until golden brown and then flip to cook the other side. Remove chicken tenders from oil and put on a paper towel lined plate to drain excess oil.

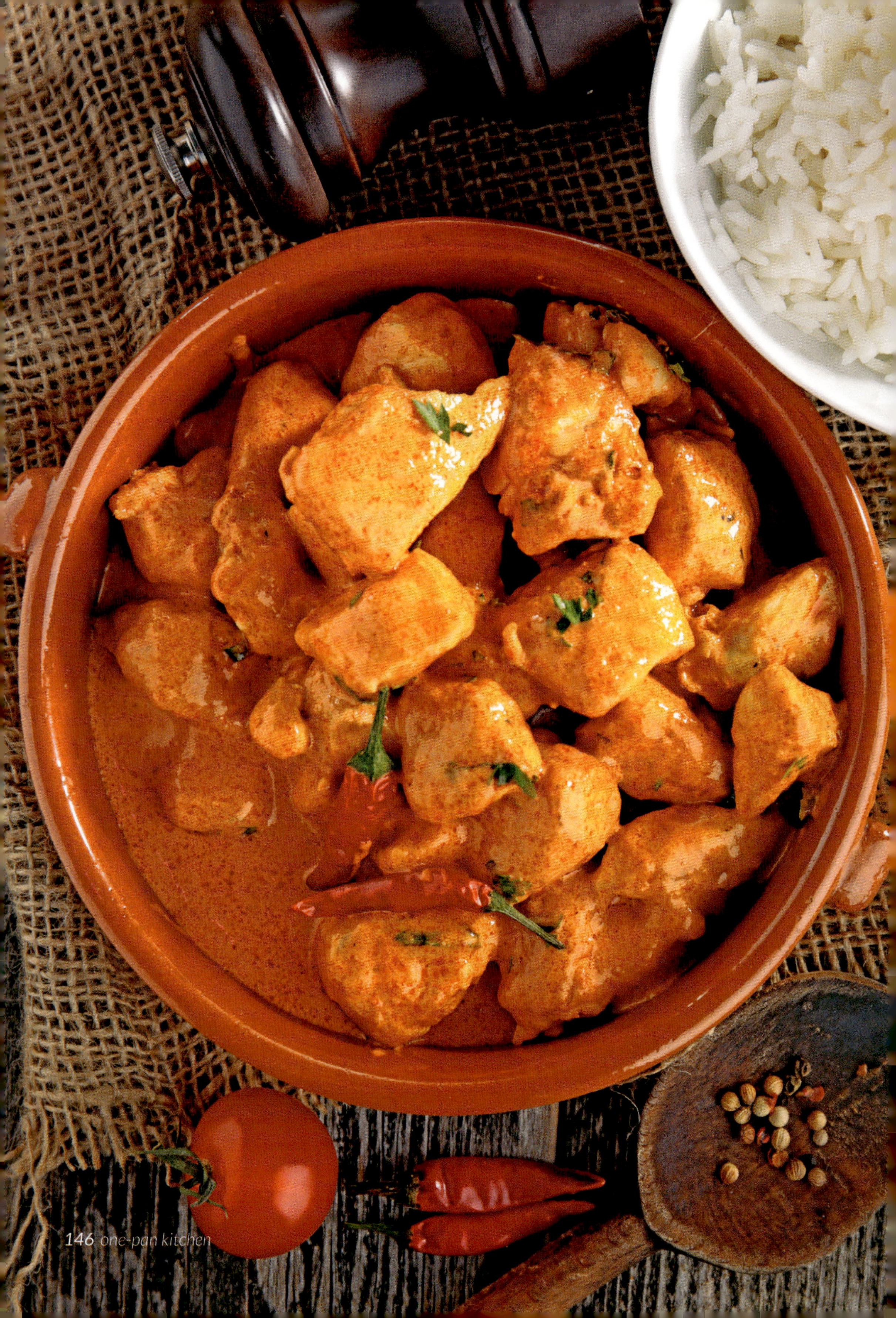

Thai Peanut Curry

Servings: 6-8   **Time:** 40 minutes

Ingredients

Curry Sauce:
¾ cup organic peanut butter
1 red bell pepper, cut
½ cup water
3 cloves garlic
2 tbsp gluten free tamari
2 tbsp Thai red curry paste
salt, to taste

Veggies and Chicken:
2 lbs boneless chicken breast, cut into 1" cubes
3 broccoli crowns (1 large bunch broccoli), cut into florets
6 medium carrots, cut diagonally into ½" thick pieces
2 cloves garlic, crushed
1 tbsp coconut oil
salt, to taste

Directions

Blend all of the curry ingredients in a blender or food processor.

Set the skillet to medium heat and fill the bottom of the pan with ¼ inch of water (if using a smaller pan, fill pan with ½ inch water).

Add carrots, garlic, and salt. Once carrots are tender, add the broccoli. Cover and steam until broccoli is cooked, but still crunchy. Uncover veggies and set aside.

Sauté chicken in coconut oil until cooked through and salt to taste. Add veggies and curry sauce to the chicken. Stir and lightly simmer for 5 minutes. Serve over rice.

Gina Picardo

"This is my dad's healthier take on one of his favorite Thai dishes. My sister and I loved it growing up and now we make it for our friends. This dish is packed with veggies and flavor, and it reheats well, making for a delicious lunch the following day."

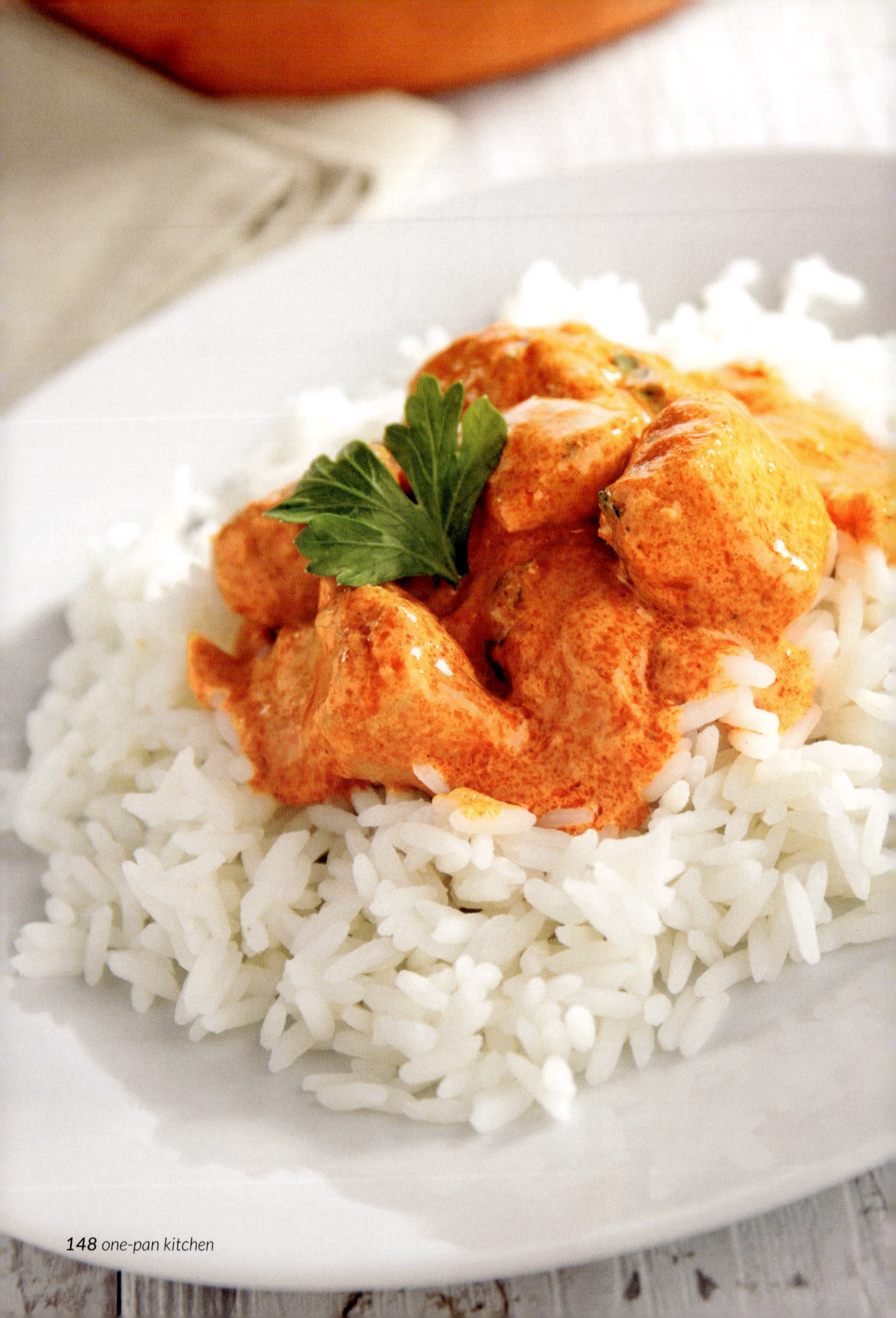

Red Curry

Servings: 4-6   **Time:** 20 minutes

Ingredients

2-3 chicken breasts, cut into chunks
1 tsp ginger, grated
2 garlic cloves, peeled and minced
1 tbsp cornstarch
1 can coconut milk
2-3 tbsp Thai red curry paste
2 tbsp fish sauce
2 tbsp cilantro, chopped
1 tbsp sesame oil

Directions

Grease skillet with sesame oil. Lightly fry ginger and garlic on medium heat until fragrant.

Add chicken breasts and cook for a few minutes on medium low heat.

Mix in red curry paste and fish sauce. Cook chicken until almost cooked through.

Mix cornstarch into coconut milk and pour over chicken. Stir and cook until chicken is fully cooked.

Serve over rice and garnish with cilantro.

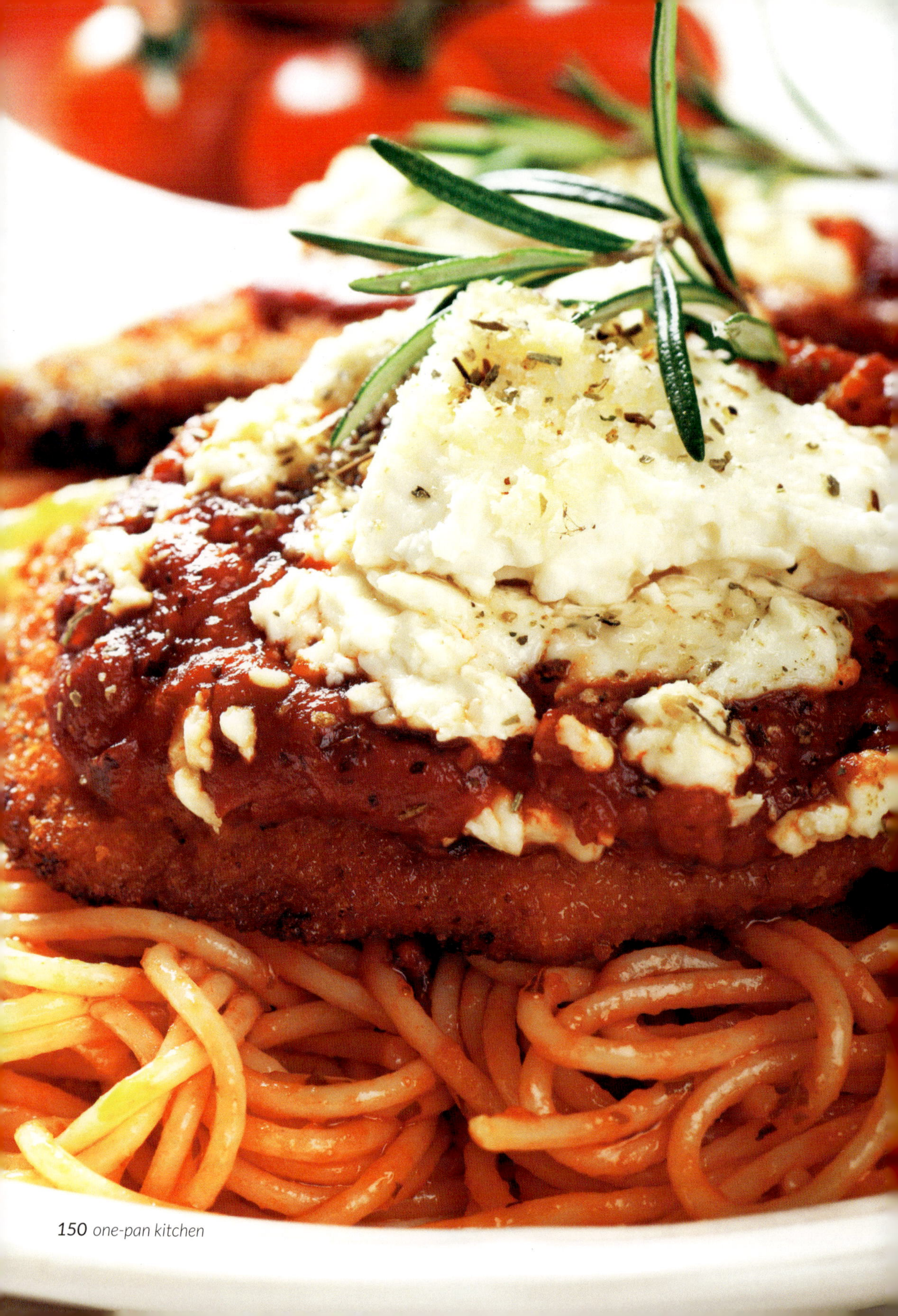

Chicken Parmigiana

Servings: 4   **Time:** 35 minutes

Ingredients

4 boneless, skinless chicken breasts
2 cups flour
1 tsp salt
½ tsp freshly ground pepper
1 tsp garlic powder
3 eggs, whisked
1½ cups panko bread crumbs
½ cup oil
8 oz fresh mozzarella, sliced
tomato sauce (see recipe, page 164)

Directions

Pound chicken breasts until thin. In a shallow dish, mix the flour with the salt, garlic, and pepper. Pour oil into the skillet and heat on high until oil shimmers. Dip chicken breasts in flour, then in egg, then in the panko bread crumbs. Fry in the skillet until golden brown on both sides.

Remove chicken breasts and pour out the oil. Place a baking rack in the skillet and set the chicken on the rack. Top each breast with a dollop of tomato sauce, a few slices of mozzarella, salt, and pepper.

Cover and finish cooking in the skillet on medium heat for 10 minutes or until the cheese is melted and the chicken is cooked through. Serve with additional tomato sauce, Parmesan cheese, and fresh herbs.

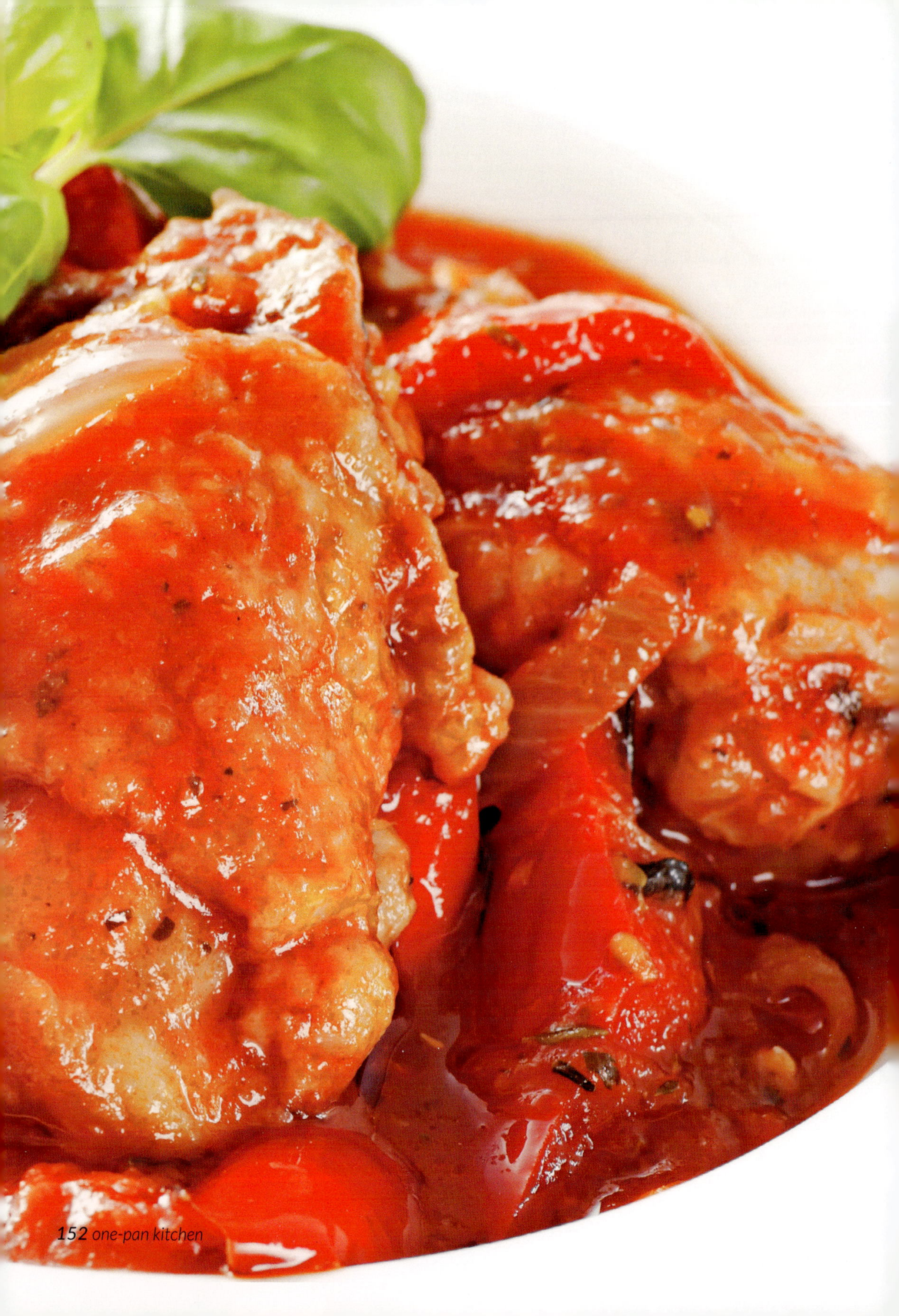

Chicken Pizzaiola

Servings: 6   **Time:** 1 hour

Ingredients

3 lbs chicken thighs

1 medium onion, diced

4 garlic cloves, minced

1 (32 oz) can crushed plum tomatoes

3 tbsp extra virgin olive oil, divided

½ tbsp Italian seasoning

¼ tsp dried oregano

¼ cup freshly grated Parmesan cheese (optional)

Directions

Preheat the skillet on medium. Add 2 tablespoons of olive oil and chicken thighs to the pan.

Brown the chicken for 3-4 minutes on each side. Reduce the heat to low.

Add the diced onion, garlic, plum tomatoes, olive oil, and seasonings. Cover and cook for 25-30 minutes, stirring every 10 minutes.

Serve over pasta, spaghetti squash, or zucchini noodles with grated Parmesan cheese, if desired.

154 one-pan kitchen

Lemon Chicken with Spinach & Mushrooms

Servings: 4-6   **Time:** 45 minutes

Ingredients

4 chicken breasts, sliced ½" thick

1 lemon

2 tbsp oregano

3 cloves garlic, minced

6 cups spinach

8 oz baby bella mushrooms, sliced

½ red onion, thinly sliced

2 cups plum tomatoes, sliced

1½ tbsp olive oil, divided

salt and pepper, to taste

Directions

Combine chicken, lemon juice, oregano, and garlic in a bowl. Season with salt and pepper and let marinate for 30 minutes.

On medium heat, lightly grease skillet with 1 tablespoon olive oil and cook chicken breasts until cooked through. Set aside.

Add mushrooms, red onion, and remaining ½ tablespoon olive oil to skillet and cook for several minutes until mushrooms begin to soften. Add spinach and cook for a few more minutes until slightly wilted. Season with salt and pepper.

Serve chicken on top of the vegetables. Garnish with tomatoes.

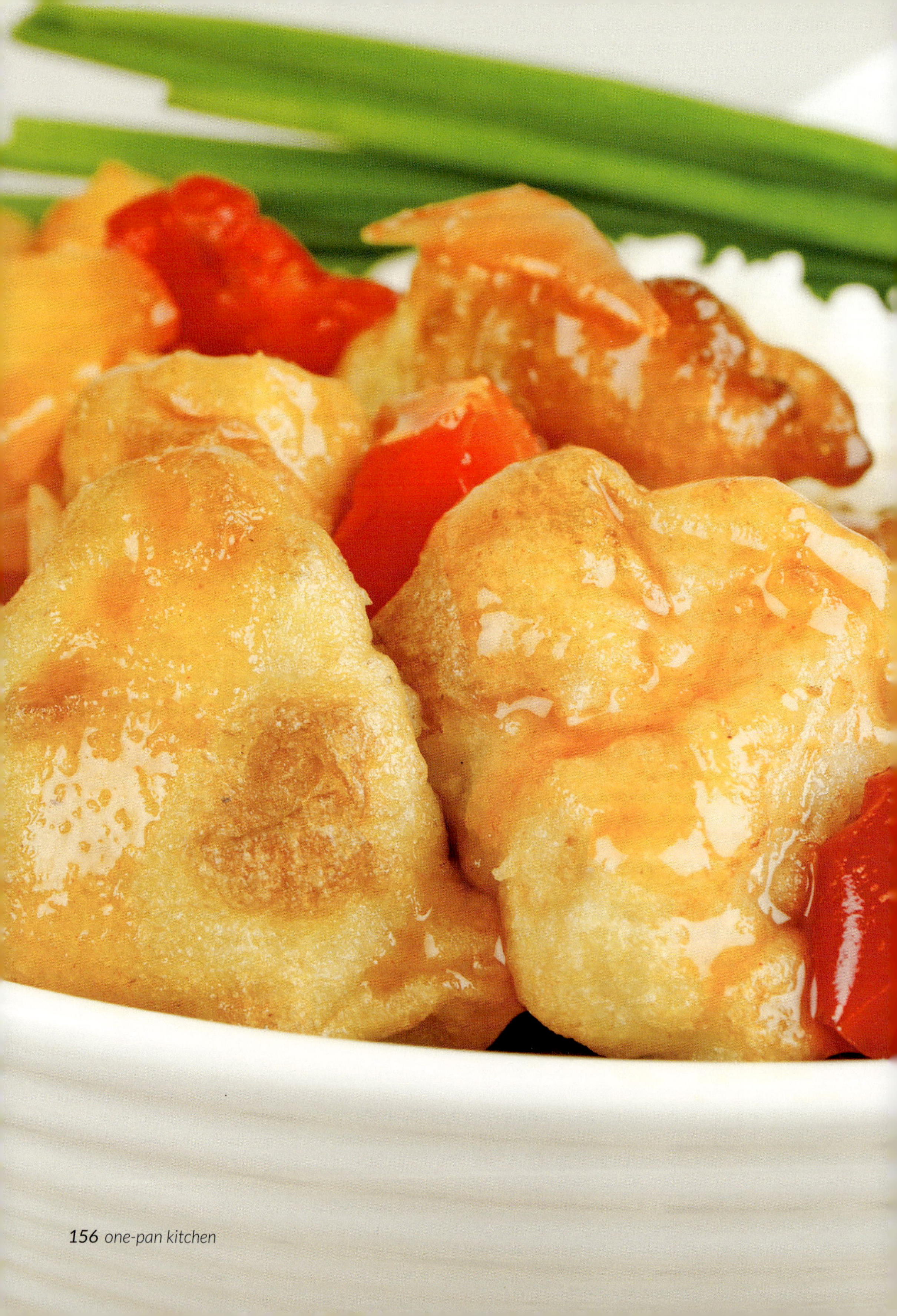

Apricot Chicken with Bell Peppers

Servings: 4   **Time:** 20 minutes

Ingredients

1 lb boneless, skinless chicken breast, cut into small pieces

1 red bell pepper, diced

¼ cup apricot jam or marmalade

2 tbsp coconut oil

salt and pepper, to taste

Directions

Lightly grease pan with the coconut oil. Start cooking chicken on medium heat. Season with salt and pepper.

When chicken is almost done, add the bell peppers and apricot jam. Cook for 2-3 minutes or until chicken is coated in jam.

Serve with rice and vegetables.

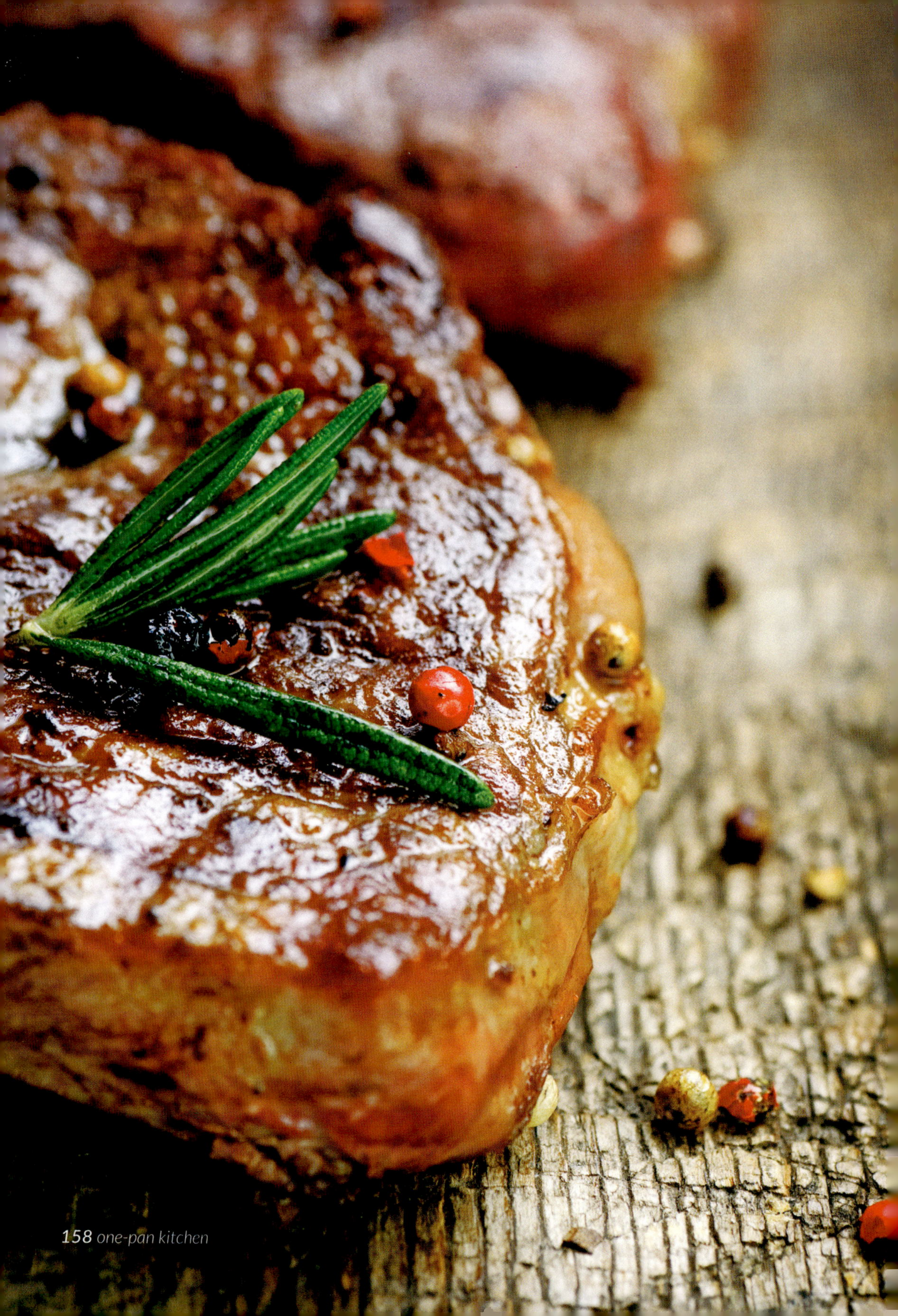

Rosemary Steak

Servings: 4   **Time:** 1 hour

Ingredients

2 strip steaks

6 garlic cloves, thinly sliced

¼ cup red wine

2 tbsp fresh rosemary

2 tbsp olive oil, divided

salt and pepper, to taste

Directions

Combine sliced garlic, red wine, rosemary, and 1 tablespoon olive oil in a dish. Marinate the steak in the mixture, flipping after 30 minutes. Season steak with salt and pepper.

Lightly grease skillet with remaining 1 tablespoon oil and cook the steak on medium heat. Flip and cook the other side until cooked to your preference.

You can also cook the marinade in the skillet and pour on top of the steak before serving.

160 one-pan kitchen

Classic Cheese Burgers

Servings: 4   **Time:** 20 minutes

Ingredients

1½ lbs ground beef

1 tbsp olive oil

½ tsp salt

¼ tsp pepper

4 slices cheddar cheese

4 hamburger buns

4 lettuce leaves

1 tomato, sliced

4 slices red onion

Directions

Divide the beef into four parts and flatten into patties. Sprinkle with salt and pepper. Heat the oil on medium and cook burgers, about 5 minutes per side. When burgers are almost done, place cheese on patties and cover with the lid.

Continue cooking until cheese melts. Place burgers on the buns and top with lettuce, tomato, red onion, and preferred condiments.

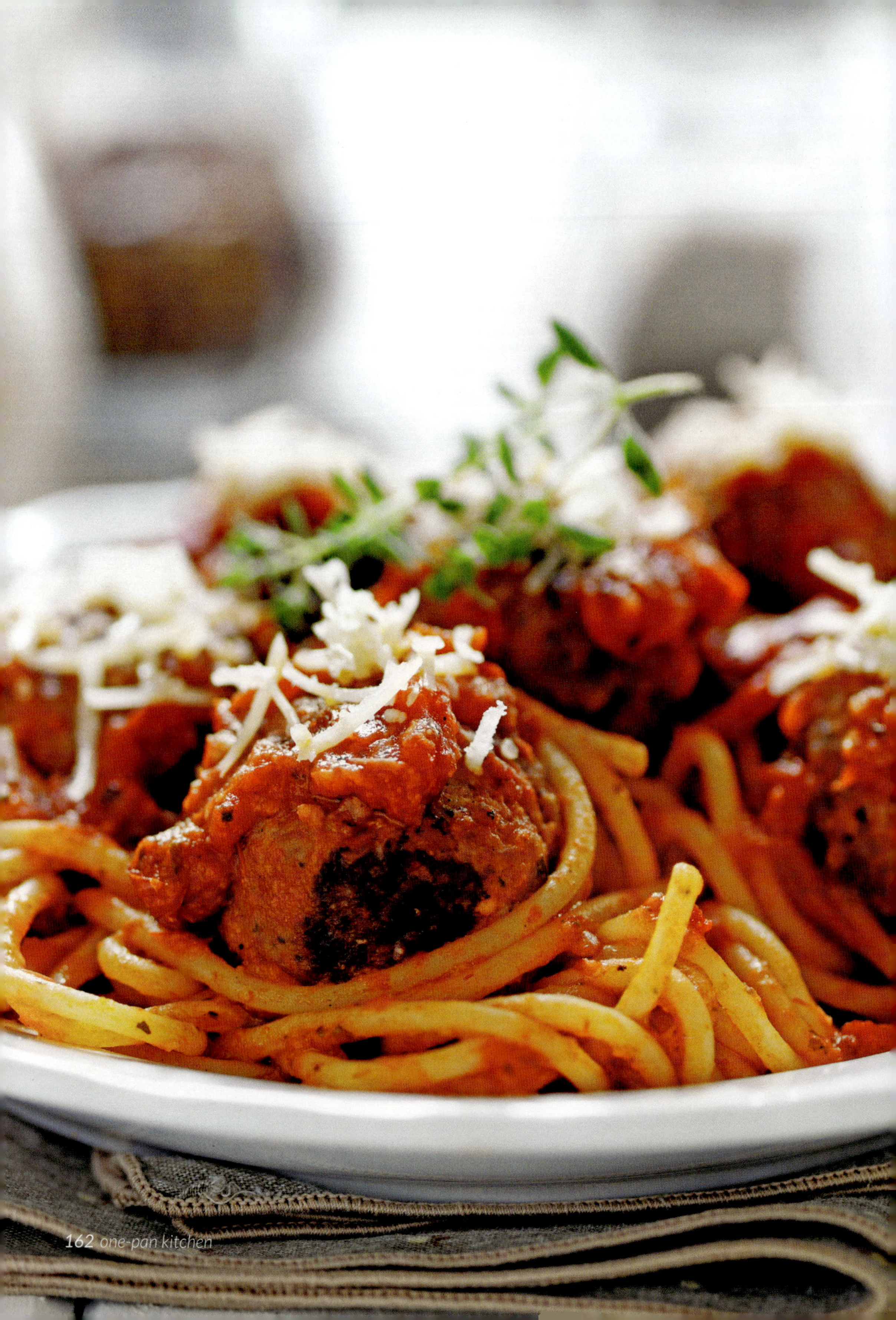

Mumma Bumma's Meatballs

Servings: 8   **Time:** 40 minutes

Ingredients

1 lb ground beef

1 lb fresh sausage, casing removed

½ fresh green pepper, diced

1 large onion, diced

1 tbsp garlic, minced

1 large egg, beaten

1 tbsp dried basil leaves

½ tsp garlic powder

½ cup Parmesan cheese, finely grated

½ cup plain breadcrumbs

1½ tbsp olive oil

Directions

In a large bowl, mix dried basil, garlic powder, Parmesan cheese, and breadcrumbs. Add beef, sausage, egg, green pepper, onion, and garlic. Mix thoroughly with your hands until the meat is completely seasoned.

Roll mixture into 1 inch balls using your hands or a cookie scoop.

Add the olive oil and the meatballs to a skillet and cook on medium heat until cooked through.

Use silicone tongs or a slotted spoon to remove the meatballs and drain them on a plate covered with paper towels.

Serve with spaghetti and your sauce of choice. See page 164 for Classic Tomato Sauce.

Shaun MacKenzie

"This is my Mom's signature dish. She never lets me go home without a big batch."

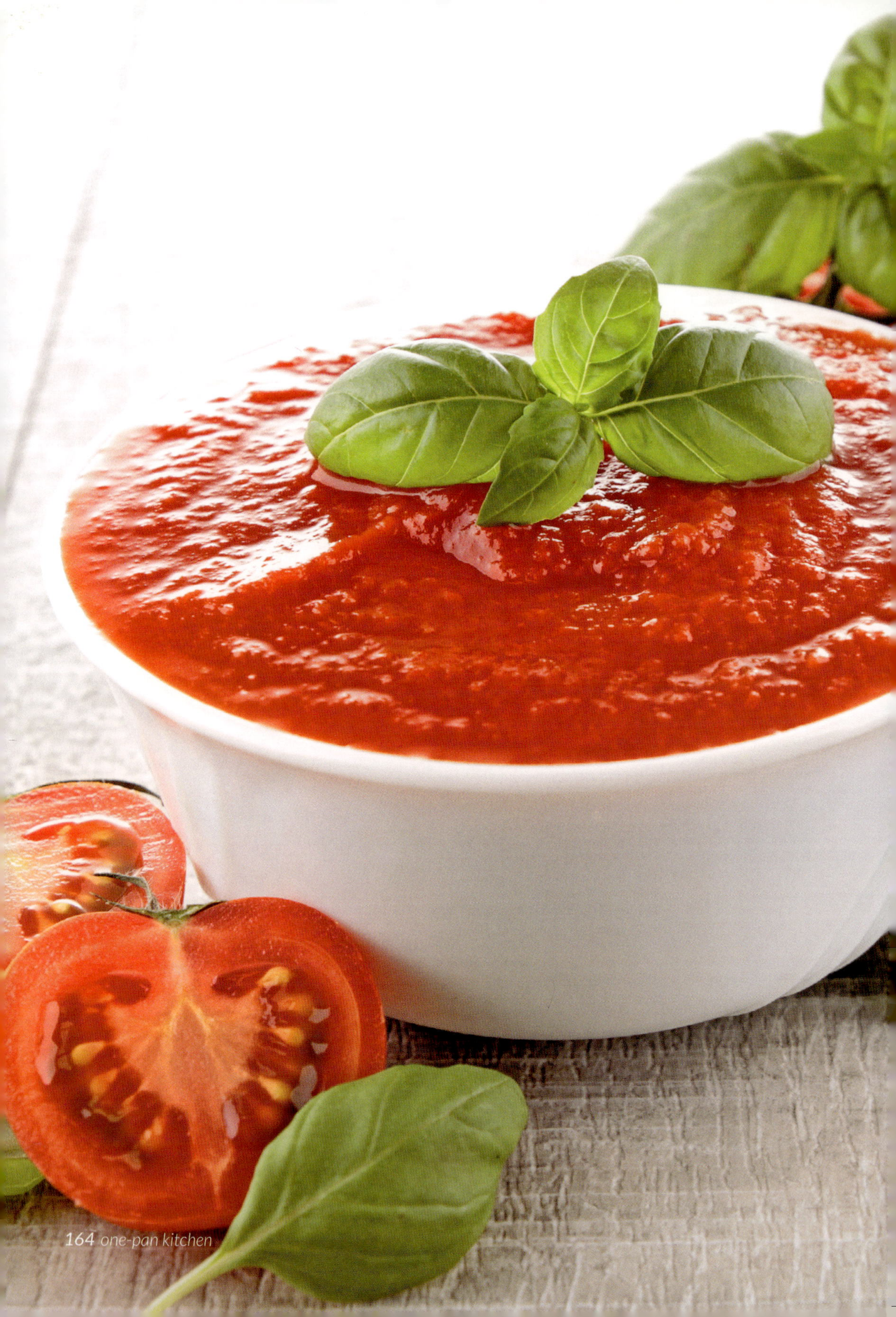

Classic Tomato Sauce

Servings: 6-8   **Time:** 30 minutes

Ingredients

2 (28 oz) cans whole Italian style plum tomatoes with basil leaf

4 cloves garlic, crushed

1 tbsp grapeseed oil

1 tsp salt

2 tsp sugar

½ tsp dried oregano

4-5 leaves fresh basil, chopped

¼ cup Italian parsley, stems removed and chopped

¼ tsp coarse black pepper

a dash of red pepper flakes

2 tbsp olive oil

Directions

On medium heat, slightly brown garlic in the grapeseed oil. Lightly crush tomatoes and add to the skillet with all remaining ingredients except for olive oil.

Bring sauce to a low simmer and cook for 20 minutes on medium low heat.

Turn off skillet and stir in olive oil.

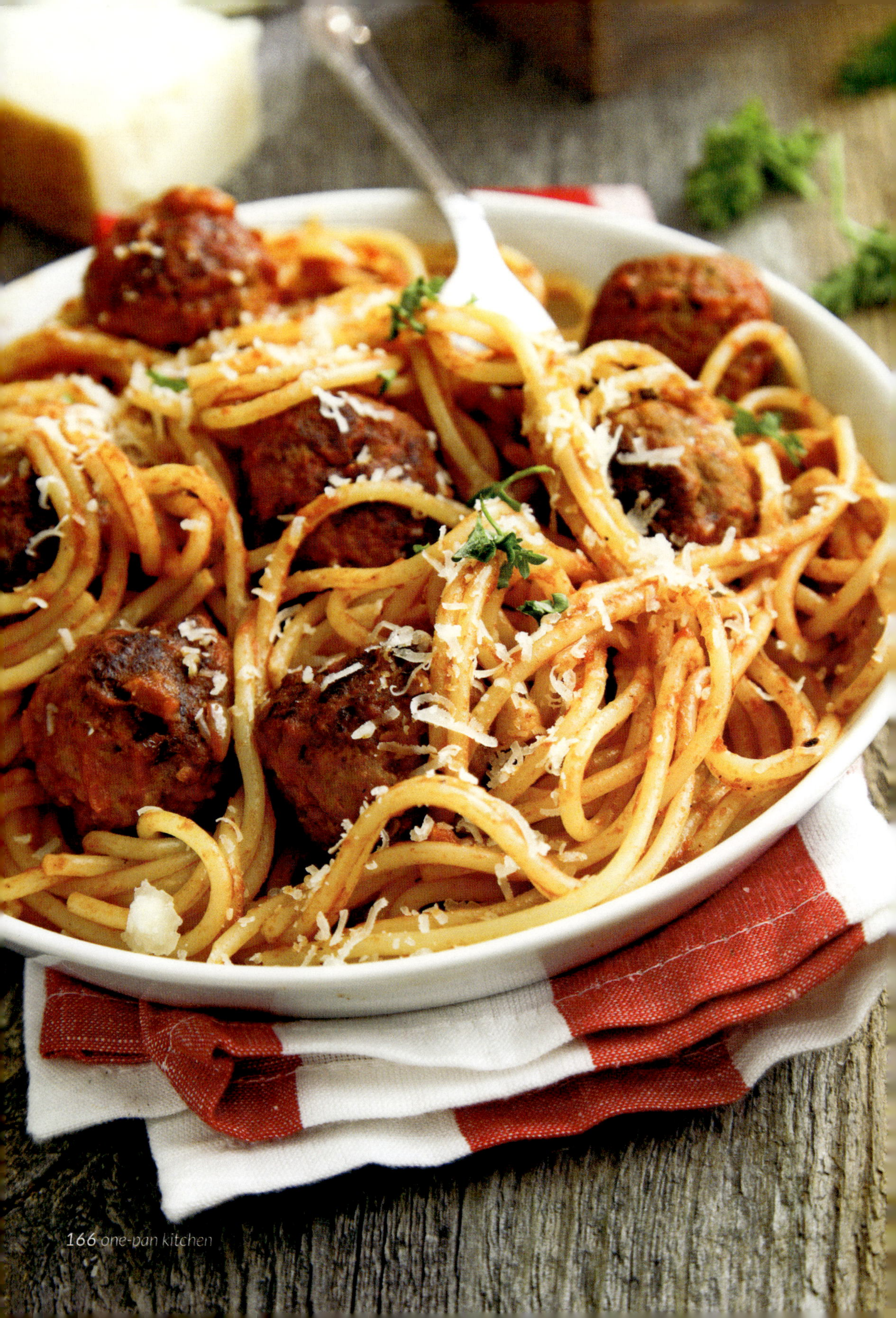

Italian Style Meatballs

Servings: 12   **Time:** 20 minutes

Ingredients

3 lbs ground beef (15-20% fat)

3 eggs

3-5 cloves garlic, crushed

1 loose cup Italian parsley, stems removed and chopped

1¼ tsp salt

1¼ cups Italian style breadcrumbs

¼ tsp coarse black pepper

¾ cup grated Romano cheese

2 tbsp extra virgin olive oil

Directions

Beat the eggs in a large bowl. Stir in the garlic, parsley, salt, and pepper. Add all remaining ingredients except for the olive oil and mix until well combined.

Roll mixture into balls that are about 1¾ inches in diameter. Set the skillet to medium heat and pour the olive oil in the pan. Cook the meatballs, flipping them occasionally, so that all sides are lightly browned.

Use silicone tongs or a slotted spoon to remove the meatballs and drain them on a plate covered with paper towels.

Serve in Classic Tomato Sauce (page 164).

168 one-pan kitchen

Classic Lasagna

Servings: 4-6   **Time:** 1½ hours

Ingredients

1 lb lean ground beef

3 eggs

10 cups favorite marinara sauce

1½ lbs (6 cups) mozzarella cheese, shredded

2 boxes no-boil lasagna noodles

2 lbs ricotta cheese

1 cup grated Parmesan cheese

1 bunch parsley or fresh basil, chopped (optional)

Directions

Cook beef on medium heat until brown. Stir in marinara sauce and cook until sauce begins to bubble. Reduce heat to medium low and simmer for 15 minutes. Pour the meat sauce in a bowl and set aside.

In a separate bowl, mix together ricotta, eggs, Parmesan, and parsley. Set aside. With skillet off, pour in 3 cups meat sauce and spread with a silicone spoon so that the sauce covers the bottom of the pan.

Lay noodles in pan so most of the bottom is covered (overlap noodles slightly). Top with half of ricotta mixture, 2 cups meat sauce, and 2 cups mozzarella. Cover with another layer of noodles. Top with remaining ricotta, 2 cups meat sauce, and 2 cups mozzarella. Finish with one more layer of noodles. Top with remaining meat sauce and mozzarella cheese.

Cover with lid and cook on low for 35-40 minutes until cheese is melted. Sprinkle with parsley, if desired. Turn the skillet off and let sit at least 30 minutes before serving.

Firehouse Chili

Servings: 8-10 **Time:** 1 hour

Ingredients

3 lbs ground beef
8 strips bacon
2 (28 oz) cans chopped tomatoes
1 (28 oz) can whole peeled tomatoes
2 (15 oz) cans kidney beans, drained
4 tbsp olive oil, divided
salt and pepper, to taste
4 large onions, chopped
1 red bell pepper, chopped
2 green bell peppers, chopped
6 garlic cloves, minced
4 tbsp ground cumin
6 tbsp chili powder
1 tbsp dried oregano
1 tsp cayenne pepper
2 cups cornmeal
1 cup shredded cheese, to garnish
sour cream and tortilla chips, to garnish

Directions

Heat 2 tablespoons olive oil over medium heat. Add the beef and cook until brown. Transfer the beef to a colander to drain and set aside.

Heat the remaining 2 tablespoons of oil in the skillet over medium high heat. Add bacon and sauté until crispy. Place the bacon on a plate lined with paper towels and let cool. Chop the bacon and return to the pan with the onions, bell peppers, and garlic. Cook over medium heat until the onions are translucent.

Stir in the cooked beef. Season with salt and pepper.

Add the tomatoes and beans. Bring to a boil, stirring occasionally.

Evan

"I love gathering friends and family and making big bowls of comfort food. I use bacon to add a nice smoky flavor. Try replacing the ground beef with ground chicken or turkey for a healthier twist."

Directions continued

Reduce heat to medium low and stir in the chili powder, cumin, oregano, and cayenne pepper. Bring to a boil again, stirring occasionally.

Reduce heat to low, cover, and let simmer for 20-30 minutes.

Stir in cornmeal to achieve the desired consistency. If desired, add more chili powder or any preferred spices.

Continue to simmer for 10 minutes or until the flavors fuse.

Spoon into bowls and top with cheese, tortilla chips, and sour cream.

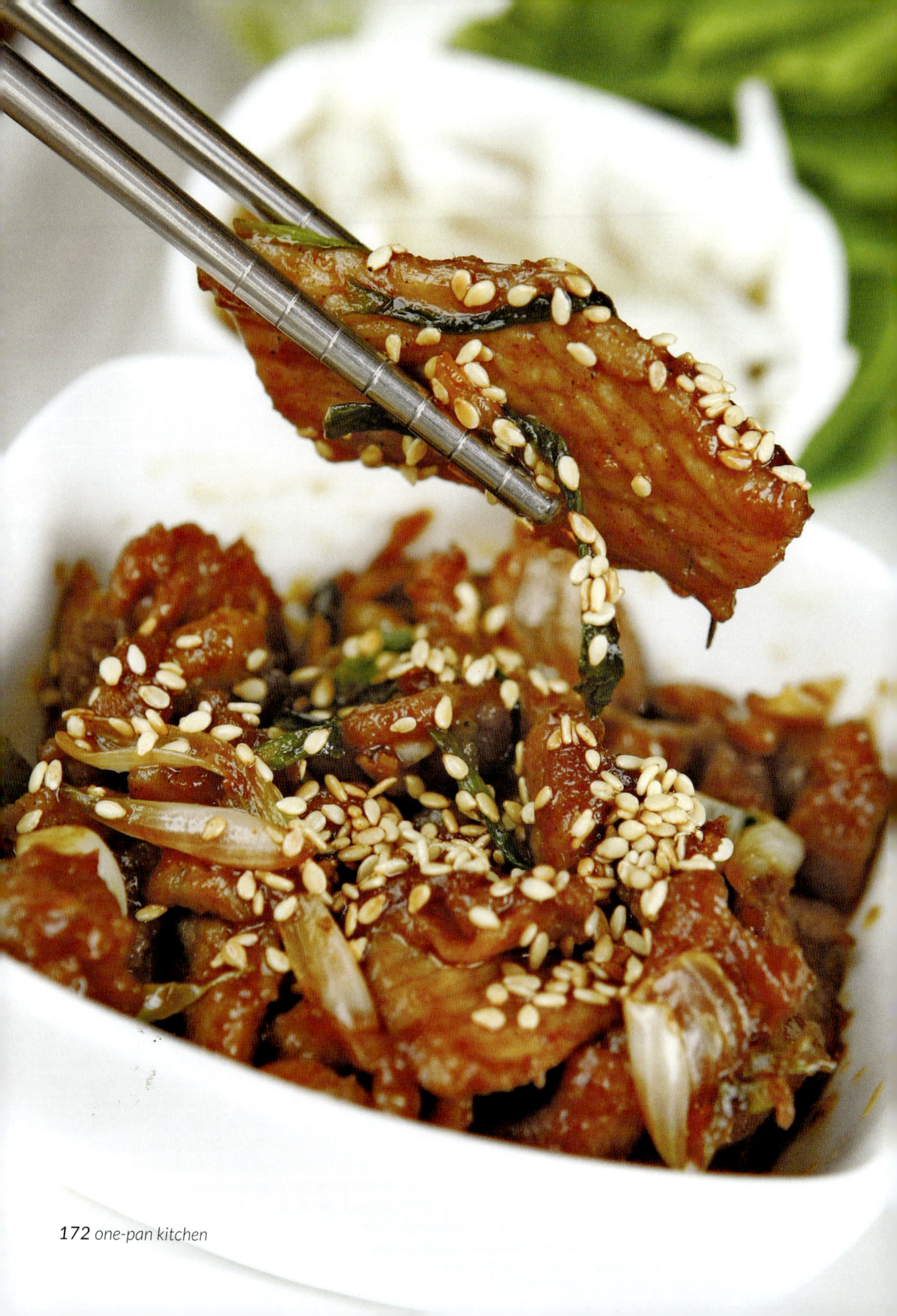

Korean BBQ Beef

Servings: 4   **Time:** 1½ hours

Ingredients

1 lb flank steak or beef tenderloin, thinly sliced

½ yellow onion, sliced

¼ cup soy sauce

2 tbsp brown sugar

½ tsp black pepper

4 cloves garlic, minced

2 green onions, chopped

1 tsp minced ginger

1 tbsp sesame oil

¼ cup crushed pear

sesame seeds, to garnish

Directions

Combine all ingredients except for beef, onions, and sesame oil in a bowl. Whisk until sugar is dissolved.

Add beef and onions to marinade and mix until meat is coated. Cover and refrigerate for at least 1 hour.

When ready to cook, lightly grease skillet with sesame oil and cook beef over high heat.

Garnish with sesame seeds. Serve with rice and vegetables.

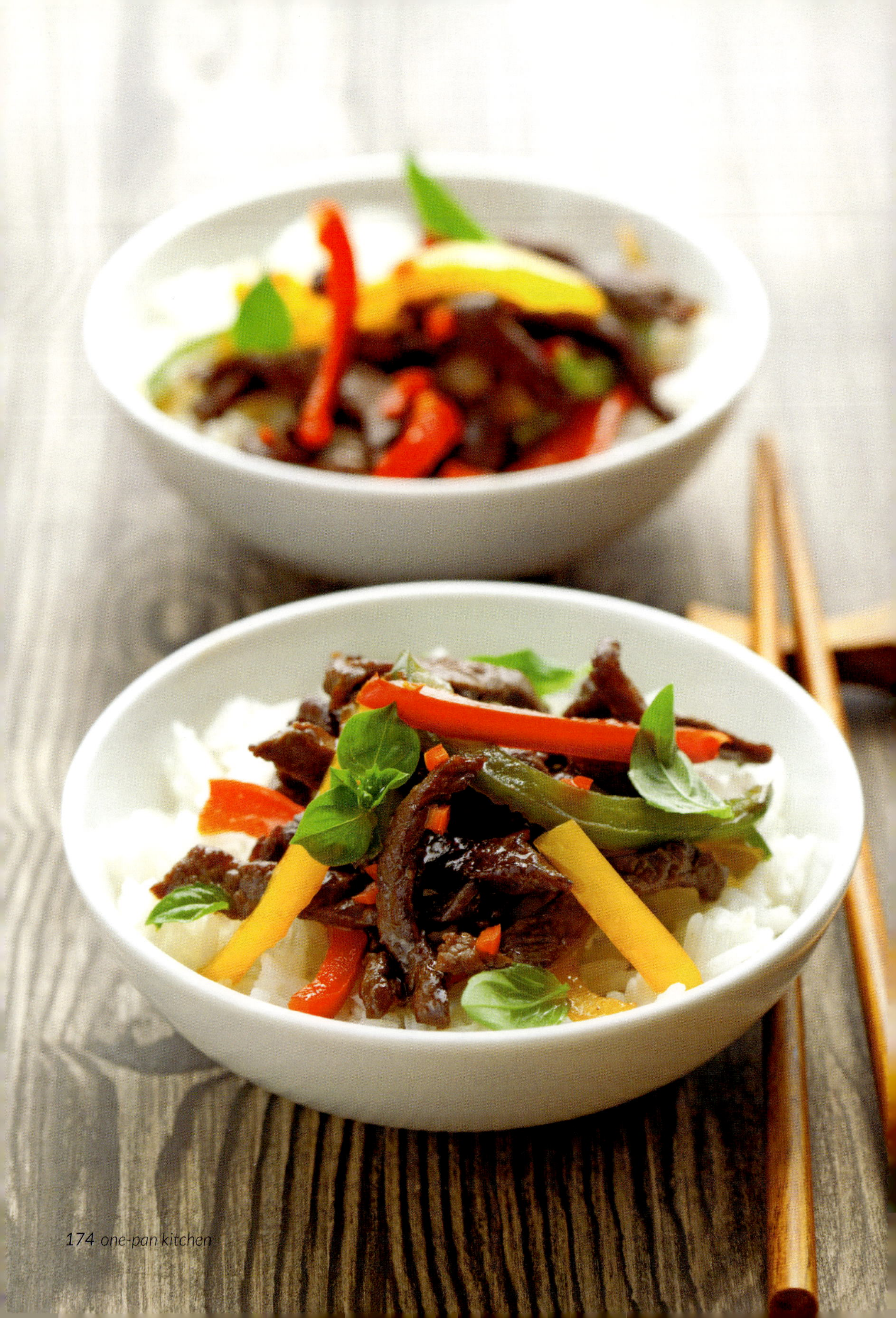

Pepper Beef

Servings: 4   **Time:** 45 minutes

Ingredients

2 shell steaks or t-bone steaks, cut into thin strips

½ tsp white pepper

2-3 cloves garlic, minced

4 tbsp soy sauce

2 tsp Worcestershire sauce

2 tsp Teriyaki sauce

½ tsp garlic powder

4 tsp olive oil, divided

1 green bell pepper, thinly sliced

1 red bell pepper, thinly sliced

1 yellow bell pepper, thinly sliced

2 medium onion, thinly sliced

salt, to taste

Directions

In a bowl, combine soy sauce, Worcestershire sauce, Teriyaki sauce, white pepper, and garlic powder. Marinate steak in mixture for 30 minutes. Season with salt.

Grease skillet with 2 teaspoons olive oil. Add garlic and steak. Cook on medium heat until steak is lightly brown and then remove from pan.

Heat the remaining olive oil in the skillet. Add onions and peppers. Cover and cook until peppers are tender. Return steak to skillet. Pour remaining marinade into skillet and stir fry together. Serve over rice.

Florence Ko

"This recipe brings me back to my childhood. My mom made this dish every Sunday for dinner because it was a family favorite."

176 one-pan kitchen

Pear & Ginger Pork

Servings: 4   **Time:** 30 minutes

Ingredients

1 lb pork tenderloin, thinly sliced

¼ cup soy sauce

3 tbsp honey

1 tbsp rice wine vinegar

¼ tsp crushed red pepper

1 tbsp extra virgin olive oil

3 medium pears, cored and sliced

1 tbsp fresh ginger, grated

½ medium yellow onion, chopped

2½ cups radicchio, chopped

2 sliced green onions, to garnish

¼ cup sliced almonds, to garnish

Directions

In a bowl, combine soy sauce, honey, rice wine vinegar, and crushed red pepper. Mix and set aside.

In a skillet, heat olive oil over medium heat. Add the pears and ginger. Cook for 2-3 minutes or until the pears soften. Remove from skillet and set aside.

Add the pork and onion to the skillet and cook for 2-3 minutes. Push the meat to the sides of the skillet. Add the soy sauce mixture and bring to a boil, stirring often. Once the sauce starts to thicken, return the pears to the pan. Stir in the radicchio and cook for 1-2 minutes.

Serve over rice with green onions and sliced almonds.

Jenna Lonergan

"I love Asian inspired dishes and takeout is just fattening and not good for you. This is an awesome, healthy alternative that gives me that sweet and salty taste when I need it! So easy to make and delicious every time. It is a staple in our house in both the summer and winter!"

entrées

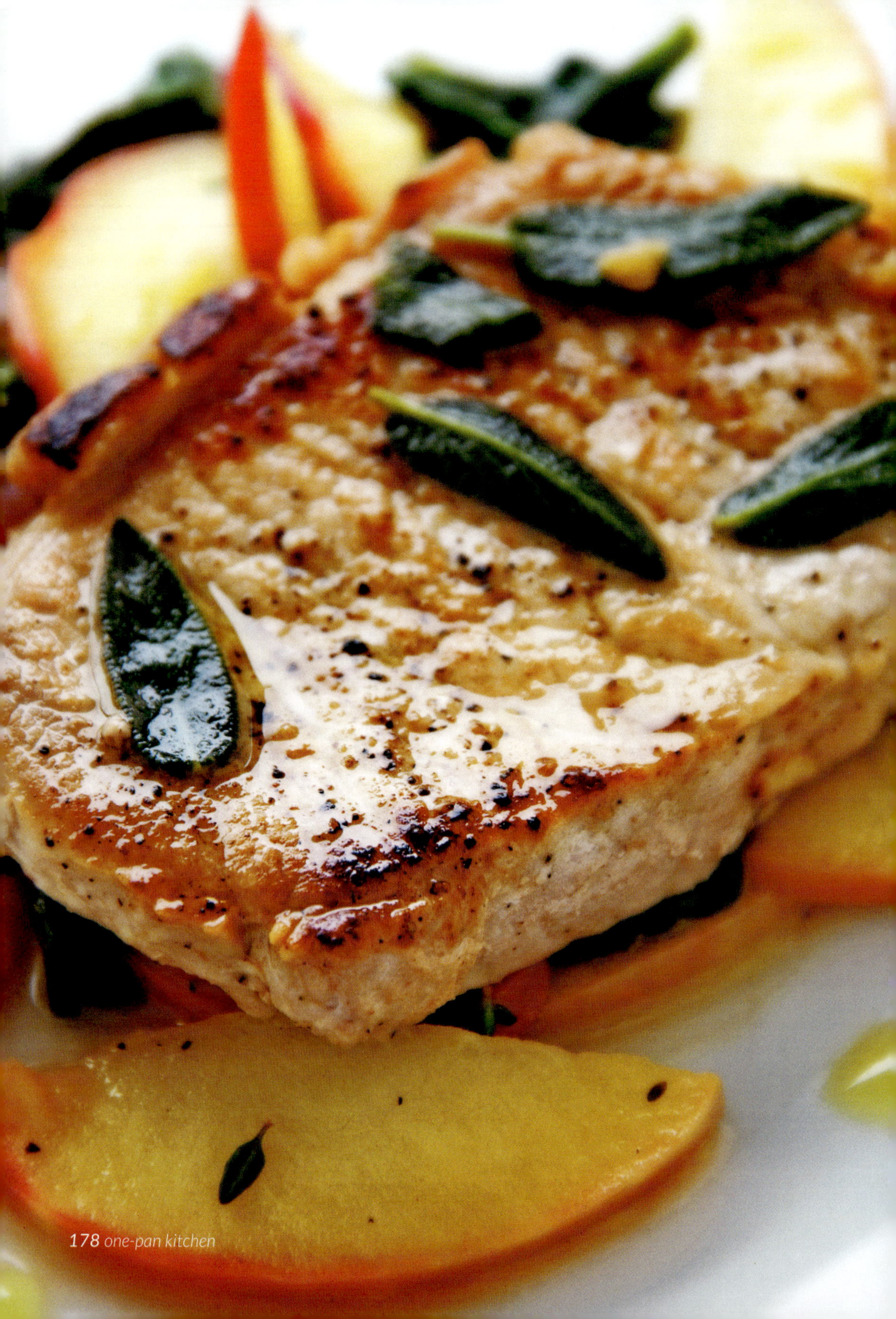

Pork Chops With Apple Gravy

Servings: 6   **Time:** 20 minutes

Ingredients

6 bone-in, center cut, thick pork chops

2 tbsp olive oil

1 tbsp brown sugar

1 tsp salt

1 tsp paprika

2 apples, cored and sliced

1 red onion, peeled and cut into wedges

1 cup pork gravy (homemade or store-bought)

1 cup apple juice or apple cider

8 sage leaves

Directions

Combine sugar, spices, and oil. Rub spices over pork chops. Set skillet to medium heat and sear pork chops on one side until golden brown.

Flip over and add apples, sage, and onion. Cook for about 3 minutes until apples are softened and pork is golden brown. Add gravy and apple juice to skillet and cover with lid. Cook until sauce begins to bubble (about 3 minutes).

Serve with potatoes and vegetables.

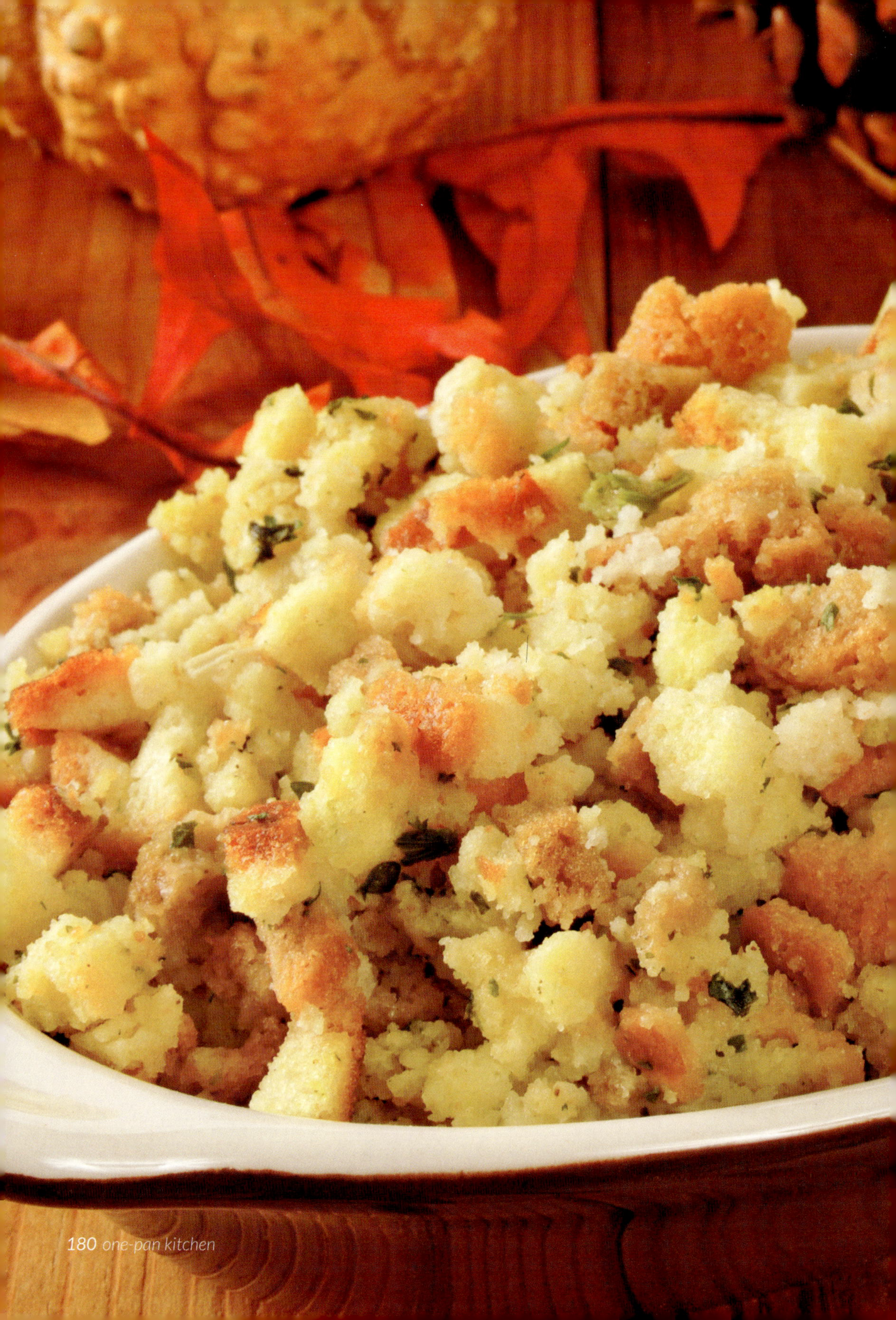

Hearty Cornbread Dressing

Servings: 6-8   **Time:** 40 minutes

Ingredients

2 (3 oz) links sweet Italian pork sausage, diced

8 cups of cornbread, cubed and dried overnight

2 medium yellow onions, diced

10 crimini (baby portabella) mushrooms, sliced

3 stalks celery, diced

2 garlic cloves, minced

2 tbsp olive oil

12 sage leaves, finely chopped

2 sprigs rosemary, finely chopped

½ cup walnut or pecan pieces

2-3 cups chicken broth

Directions

Preheat the skillet on low heat and add the olive oil. After 10 seconds, add the diced onions, celery, and garlic. Stir for 1 minute and add the mushrooms. Cook until the onions and celery soften (about 3 minutes).

Stir in the diced sausage and cook for 3-4 minutes. Add the nuts and herbs and toast for 30 seconds. Pour the mixture into a large mixing bowl with the cornbread. Pour 1 cup of the chicken broth over the cornbread and vegetables. Mix with your hands, adding ½ cup of broth at a time until the cornbread is completely saturated but not dripping wet.

Set the skillet to low heat and return the mixture to the pan. Cover and cook for 10 minutes. Remove the cover and fold the dressing so that the top is now on the bottom of the pan. Cover and cook for another 5 minutes. Serve warm.

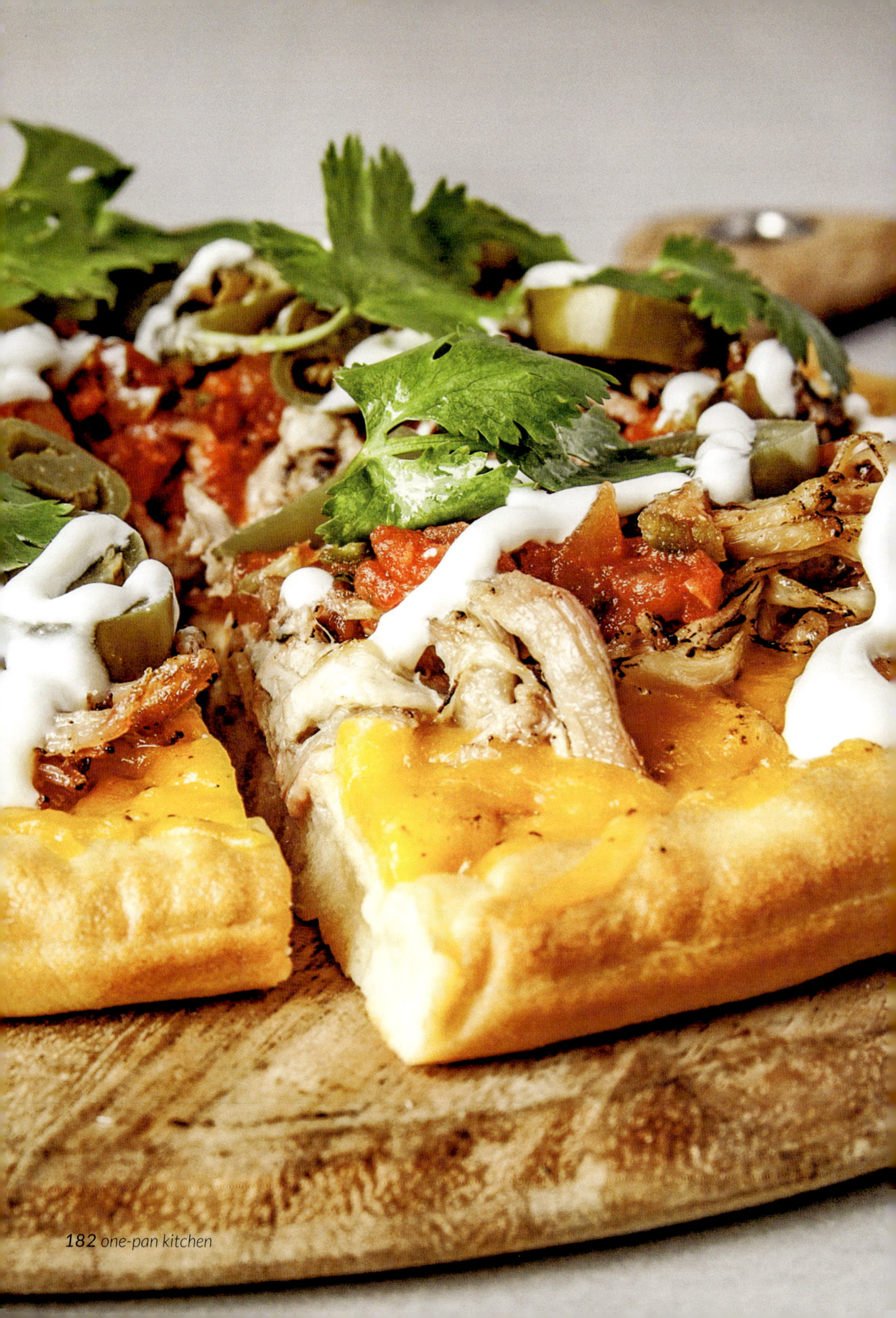

Carnitas Pizza

Servings: 8-12 **Time:** 4-5 hours

Ingredients

3-4 lbs chuck roast

2 tsp chili powder

1 tsp cumin

1 tsp oregano

1 tsp kosher salt

3½ tbsp olive oil, divided

3 cups pineapple juice

1 store-bought or homemade raw pizza dough

1 cup jarred tomatillo salsa

2 cups fresh mozzarella, thinly sliced

1 onion, thinly sliced

1 red bell pepper, thinly sliced

3 green onions, sliced

Directions

Mix together 2 tablespoons oil and spices and rub over chuck roast. Set skillet to medium and sear roast on both sides. Then, add pineapple juice, cover with lid, and set heat to low. Cook meat for 3-4 hours until it can be easily shredded. Remove meat, shred, and set aside. Set skillet to low. Add sliced peppers and onions and cook, stirring often, until caramelized. Remove and set aside. Wipe out the skillet.

Roll dough into a 14 inch diameter. Turn skillet to low and brush bottom with 1 tablespoon oil. Place dough in skillet and cook about 3-4 minutes until bottom is browned. Brush the top of the dough with ½ tablespoon olive oil and flip it over. Top with tomatillo salsa, mozzarella slices, caramelized onions and peppers, and shredded meat. Sprinkle with green onions. Place lid on skillet and cook about 5 minutes or until cheese is melted. Serve with guacamole and sour cream, if desired.

Eggplant Parmigiana

Servings: 10-12   **Time:** 1 hour

Ingredients

3 large eggplant, sliced into ¼" rounds

5 eggs

1 cup kosher salt (for salting the eggplant)

6 cups breadcrumbs, cornmeal or gluten-free breadcrumbs

1 tbsp freshly ground black pepper

1 tbsp dried basil

64 oz marinara sauce

1 cup shredded parmesan cheese

16 oz (2 balls) fresh mozzarella, thinly sliced

1 cup olive oil

fresh basil, to garnish

Directions

Lay the eggplant out on paper towels and cover each piece with kosher salt. Let the eggplant sit for 1-2 hours and then rinse each slice under cold water. Press the eggplant rounds between paper towels to remove any moisture.

Whisk eggs in a medium-sized mixing bowl. In a second bowl, mix the breadcrumbs, dried basil, and black pepper. Fill the bottom of your skillet with a thin layer of oil and heat on medium.

Dip each eggplant slice into the egg and then into the breadcrumb mixture. Put each slice directly into the pan, working around the pan until it is filled but not crowded. Cook eggplant for 3-4 minutes on each side until the breadcrumbs are golden brown. Add oil, one tablespoon at a time, to the pan, as necessary. Remove the slices from the pan and set onto a baking sheet lined with paper towels to absorb any excess oil.

Catherine-Gail Reinhard

"To me, there's no better crowd pleaser than Eggplant Parm. It's one of my favorites to order at a restaurant but making it at home is much more satisfying because you know the quality of the ingredients. It's great for parties because it's vegetarian but the eggplant is still hearty and filling."

Directions continued

Continue dredging, cooking, and draining the eggplant in batches until all the eggplant slices have been cooked.

Let the skillet cool and then wipe clean. Cover the bottom of the skillet with a layer of marinara sauce and then add a layer of eggplant.

Sprinkle shredded Parmesan over each piece of eggplant and then add a tablespoon of sauce and a slice of mozzarella. Add another layer of eggplant on top of the mozzarella and then top with shredded Parmesan and the remaining sauce. Top each round of eggplant with a slice of mozzarella. Cover the skillet and turn the heat to low. Cook for 20–25 minutes. Uncover and cook for 5 more minutes. Let sit for 15 minutes. Garnish with fresh basil leaves and serve.

Korean Stir-Fried Noodles (Japchae)

Servings: 6-8　　**Time:** 1½ hours

Ingredients

1 lb sweet potato noodles (dangmyeon), pre-cut

3 eggs

2-3 tbsp olive oil, divided

2 tbsp sesame oil, divided

¼ cup soy sauce, divided

2 tbsp sugar, divided

1 cup carrots, thinly sliced

1 cup red onion, julienned

1 red bell pepper, sliced

4 dried shiitake mushrooms

1 bunch spinach, blanched

1 tbsp garlic, minced

toasted sesame seeds, to garnish

salt and pepper, to taste

Directions

Soak shiitake mushrooms in water for 1 hour. Rinse and julienne.

In a small bowl, mix 2 tablespoons soy sauce with 1 tablespoon sugar.

In a skillet, bring water to a boil on high heat. Add noodles, stirring occasionally for 5 minutes.

Drain noodles and place in a large bowl. Add soy sauce and sugar mixture and 1 tablespoon sesame oil. Toss to coat the noodles and set aside.

Lightly grease the pan with olive oil. Over medium heat, add onions and bell peppers. Season with salt and lightly stir-fry until they are cooked but still crisp. Remove from pan and set aside. Repeat with the carrots and set aside.

Sunny Choi

"This recipe is a very traditional (and delicious) Korean dish that my mom makes for holidays, family birthdays, and other special occasions. It's one of my favorites and I hope you enjoy it too!"

Directions continued

Beat eggs in a bowl. Lightly grease the skillet over medium low heat and add eggs. Once the bottom is cooked through, roll egg into a long, thin cylinder. Remove from pan, slice, and set aside.

Add olive oil and stir-fry mushrooms over medium heat. Then, add garlic and stir. Chop blanched spinach into smaller pieces. Once mushrooms are tender, add spinach and lightly stir-fry until warm. Season with salt to taste.

Add noodles, cooked vegetables, and 1 tablespoon sesame oil to skillet. Stir-fry until warm. Add soy sauce and sugar in a 2:1 ratio until the noodles are seasoned to your liking. Season with black pepper.

Remove from heat and garnish with egg and toasted sesame seeds.

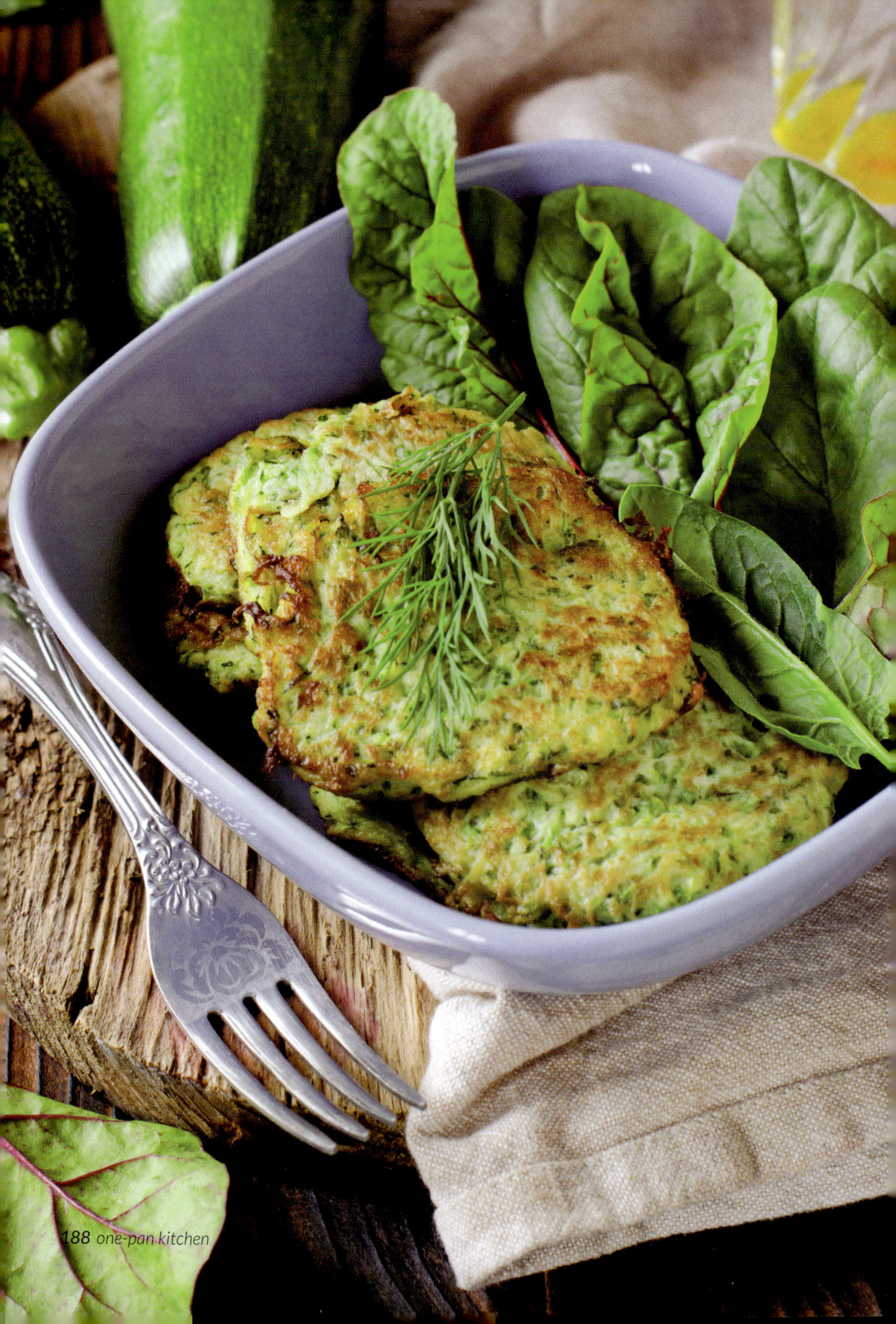

Zucchini Burgers

Servings: 8   **Time:** 20 minutes

Ingredients

4 small zucchinis, shredded (about 4 cups)

1½ cup corn

4 tbsp almond butter

2 eggs

1 cup flour

2 tsp garlic powder

4 tsp onion powder

1 tsp salt

2 tsp paprika

3 tbsp olive oil

Directions

Squeeze the shredded zucchini in paper towels to get rid of excess moisture. In a bowl, combine zucchini, almond butter, egg, and corn. In another bowl, add the flour, garlic powder, onion powder, salt, and paprika.

Pour dry ingredients over zucchini mixture and mix well. Heat olive oil in the skillet on medium high heat. Shape zucchini mixture into eight patties and cook until golden and crisp.

Serve on hamburger buns or on a bed of mixed greens.

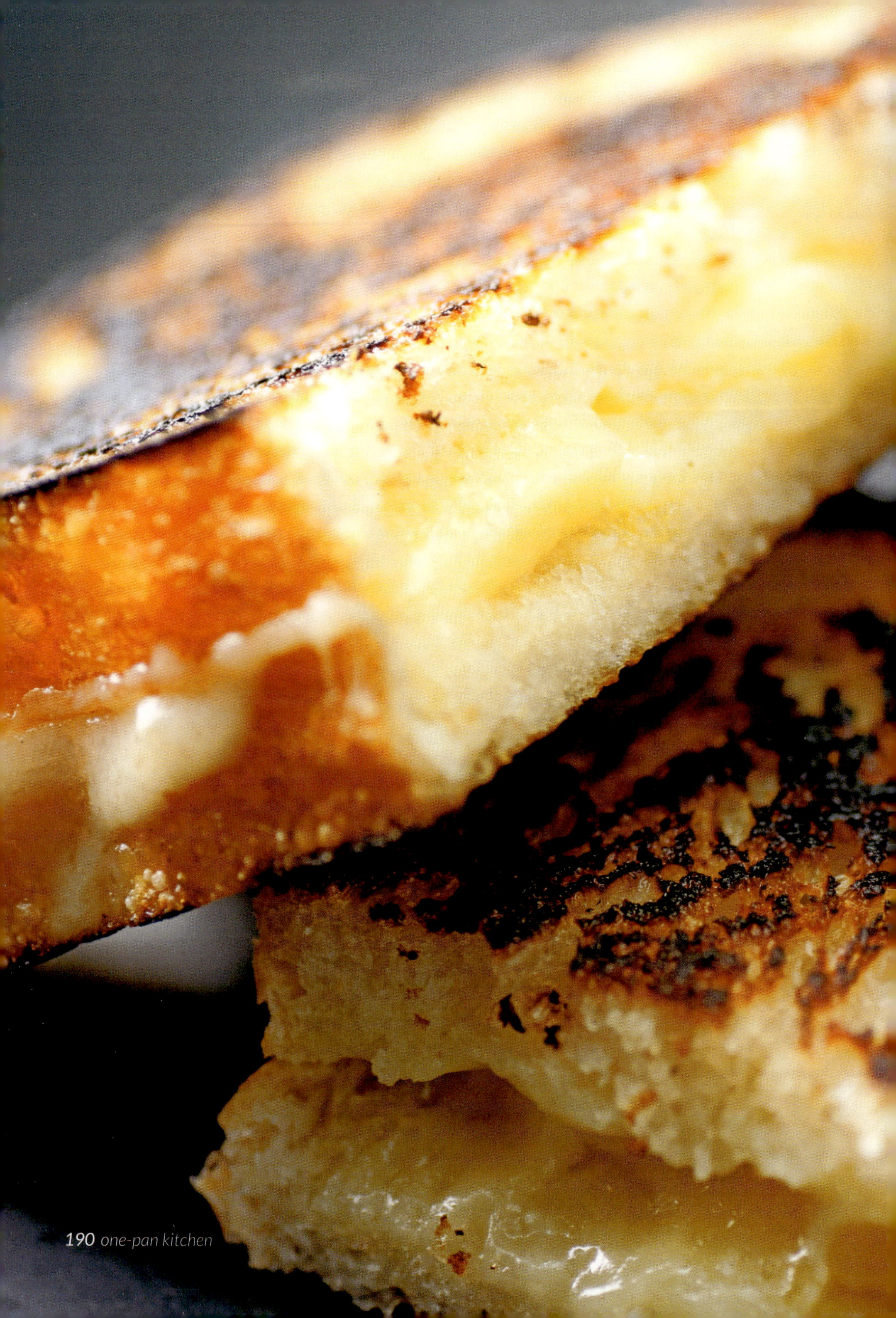

Gourmet Grilled Cheese

Servings: 4

Time: 15 minutes

Ingredients

8 slices good quality bread

8 slices Monterey Jack cheese

8 slices Swiss cheese

4 tbsp butter, room temperature

Directions

Butter one side of each slice of bread. Place 4 slices, buttered side down, in a skillet set to medium heat. Layer two pieces of Swiss and Monterey Jack cheese on each slice of bread and top with another slice of bread, buttered side up.

Once the bread has browned and the cheese has started to melt, flip the sandwich over and brown the other side. Serve warm.

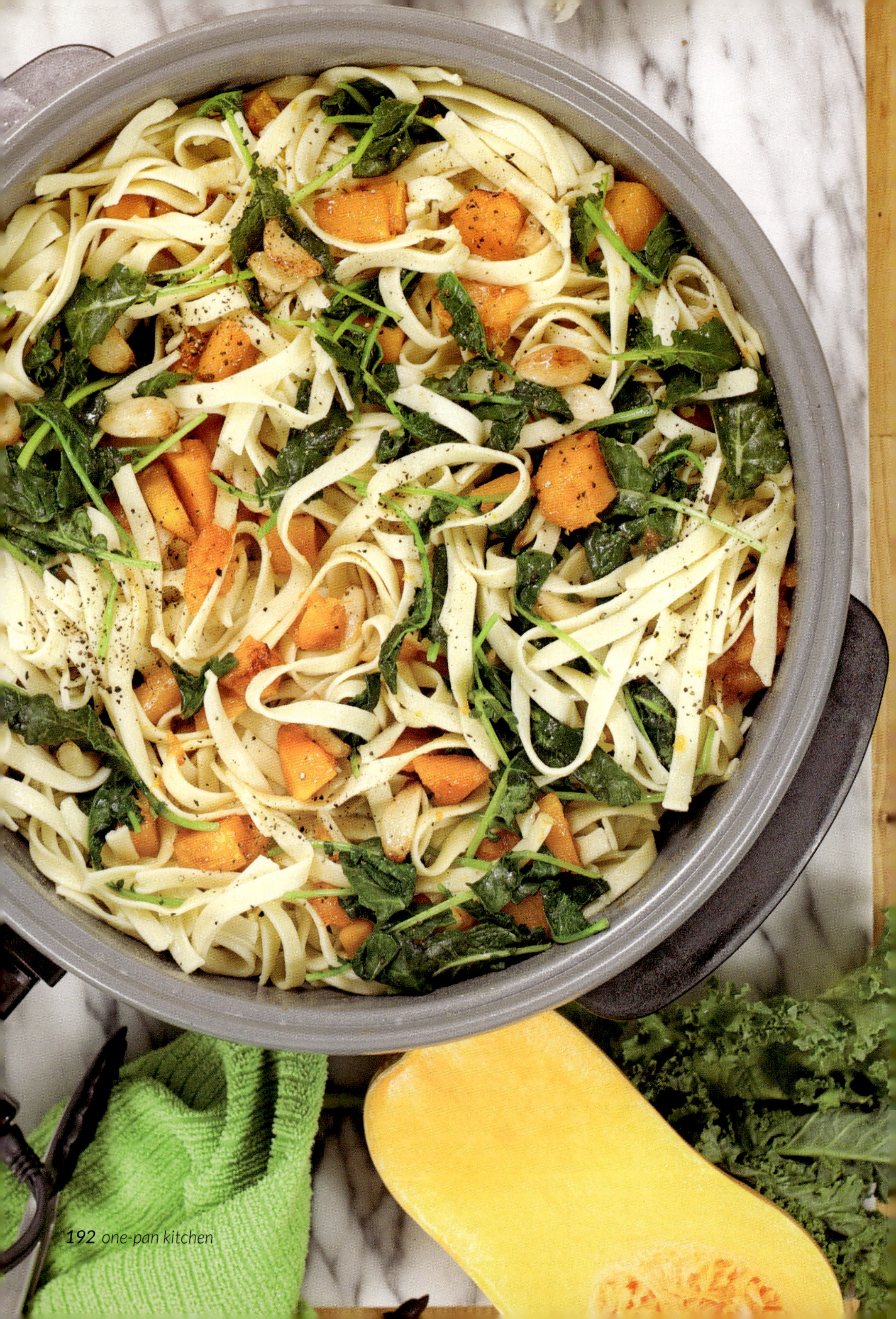

Butternut Squash & Kale Linguine

Servings: 4   **Time:** 1½ hours

Ingredients

½ lb linguine

1 bunch kale, stems removed and chopped

2 tbsp olive oil

½ cup white wine

¼ tsp ground nutmeg

1 tbsp fresh sage, chopped

½ butternut squash, cut into 1" cubes

½ tsp coarse black pepper

2 tsp salt

¼ cup Parmigiano Reggiano

2 cloves garlic, minced

Directions

Set your skillet to low or medium low heat. In the pan, sauté the garlic in olive oil.

Add the wine, nutmeg, pepper, and butternut squash. Mix so that the squash is lightly coated in the liquid. Cover with lid and cook for 30-35 minutes or until tender, stirring every now and then.

Mix in the kale and re-cover for another 10 minutes, stirring occasionally. Pour into a bowl and cover with a dish cloth.

Allow your skillet to cool, then clean it. Fill with 2-3 quarts of water and add salt. Set skillet to high and bring the water to a boil. Add pasta and cook for about 9 minutes, stirring frequently. Drain the pasta and then return it to the skillet over low heat. Stir in the squash and kale. Mix in the cheese and sage and serve.

Sweet Potato Pancakes   pg 206-207

Sides

196-197 Garlic Broccoli

198-199 Pan-Seared Brussel Sprouts

200-201 Pine Nut and Ginger Broccoli

202-203 Sautéed Root Vegetables

204-205 Potato Pancakes

206-207 Sweet Potato Pancakes

208-209 Roasted Yams with Orange Glaze

210-211 Sage Mashed Potatoes

212-213 Sourdough Stuffing

214-215 Spiced Cranberry Relish

216-217 Cinnamon Apple Sauce

218-219 Skillet Polenta

220-221 Squash Risotto

222-223 Couscous Salad

224 Steak and Strawberry Salad

225 Sweet Skillet Cornbread

226-227 Focaccia Bread

228-229 Homemade Tortillas

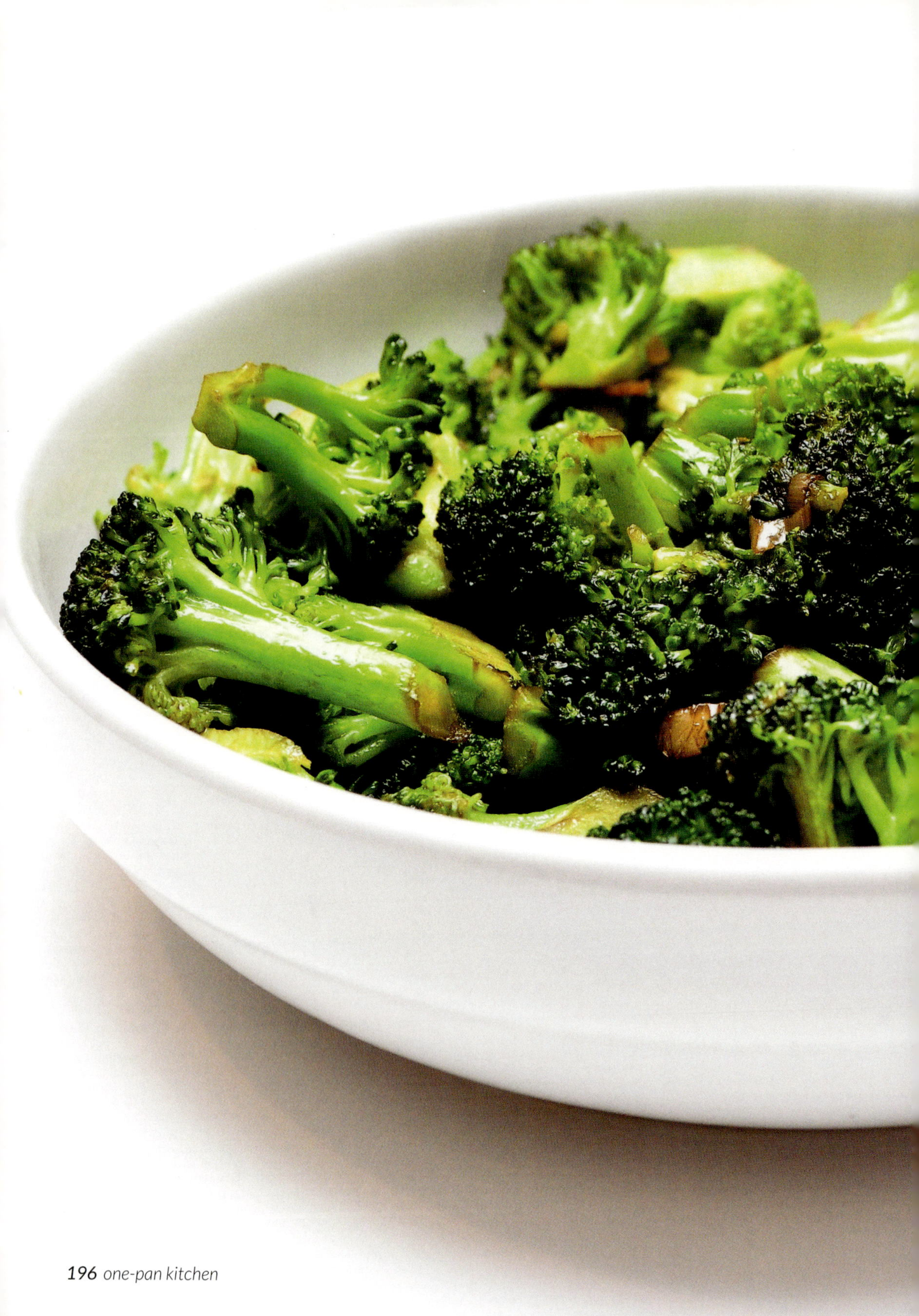

Garlic Broccoli

Servings: 4-5   **Time:** 15 minutes

Ingredients

3 crowns broccoli, sliced into florets
½ cup water
1 tsp salt
1 tsp black pepper
3 tbsp olive oil
3 cloves garlic, chopped
½ tsp red pepper flakes (optional)

Directions

Heat olive oil over medium high heat. Add garlic and red pepper flakes.

Spread out the broccoli in the pan. Season with salt and pepper. Don't stir until the broccoli has browned (about 2 minutes).

Add water, cover, and steam for 5 minutes. Uncover the skillet and stir the broccoli.

Continue to cook the broccoli without the lid until the water has cooked off and the desired doneness is reached.

198 one-pan kitchen

Pan Seared Brussels Sprouts

Servings: 4   **Time:** 10 minutes

Ingredients

1 pound Brussels sprouts, washed

2 garlic cloves, minced

4 tbsp olive oil

1 lemon

salt and pepper, to taste

Directions

Cut Brussels sprouts length wise and trim stems.

Heat olive oil in the skillet over medium high heat. Once hot, place the sprouts face down in the pan. Sprinkle the garlic over the sprouts and season with salt and pepper. Flip the sprouts once they have browned and cook the other side.

Serve with a squeeze of lemon.

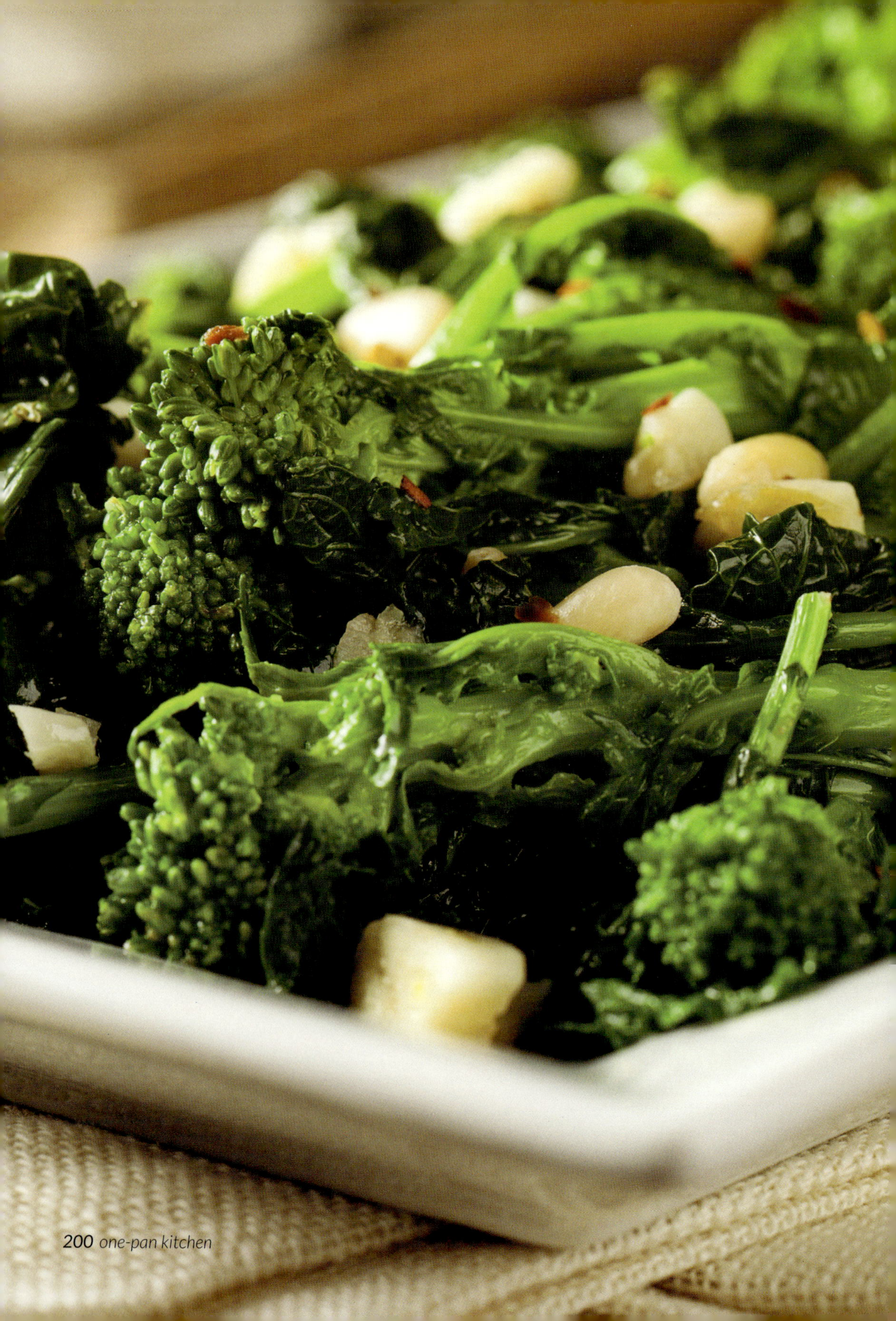

Pine Nut and Ginger Broccoli

Servings: 4-6　　**Time:** 15 minutes

Ingredients

1 lb chinese broccoli

2 tbsp pine nuts

½ cup vegetable stock

2 tbsp tamarind sauce

2 tbsp olive oil

1 clove of garlic

2 tbsp fresh ginger, minced

Directions

Toast the pine nuts in the skillet on medium until fragrant. Remove from heat and set aside.

Add the olive oil to the skillet on medium high heat. Add the garlic and ginger and sauté for 1 minute. Stir in broccoli and toss to coat in oil. Sauté for 2 more minutes.

Pour vegetable stock and tamarind sauce into the skillet. Bring liquid to a simmer, cover, and cook for 3 minutes.

Remove broccoli with a slotted spoon and place in a serving bowl. Top with toasted pine nuts. Continue to simmer sauce in the skillet until it has been reduced by half. Pour reduced sauce over broccoli and serve.

02 *one-pan kitchen*

Sautéed Root Vegetables

Servings: 4-6   **Time:** 35 minutes

Ingredients

4 carrots

3 shallots

8 garlic cloves

2 parsnips, sliced into rounds

2 small turnips

½ cup olive oil

2 sprigs rosemary, chopped

½ tsp salt

¼ tsp ground pepper

Directions

Slice carrots lengthwise and then into quarters. Cut the shallots in half. Leave the garlic cloves unpeeled. Slice the turnips into wedges.

Add the vegetables, olive oil, and seasonings to the skillet. Toss to coat.

Turn the skillet on low heat and cover. Pan roast on low for 15 minutes. Remove the lid and stir. Re-cover and continue to cook for another 10 minutes. Cook for an additional 5 minutes uncovered.

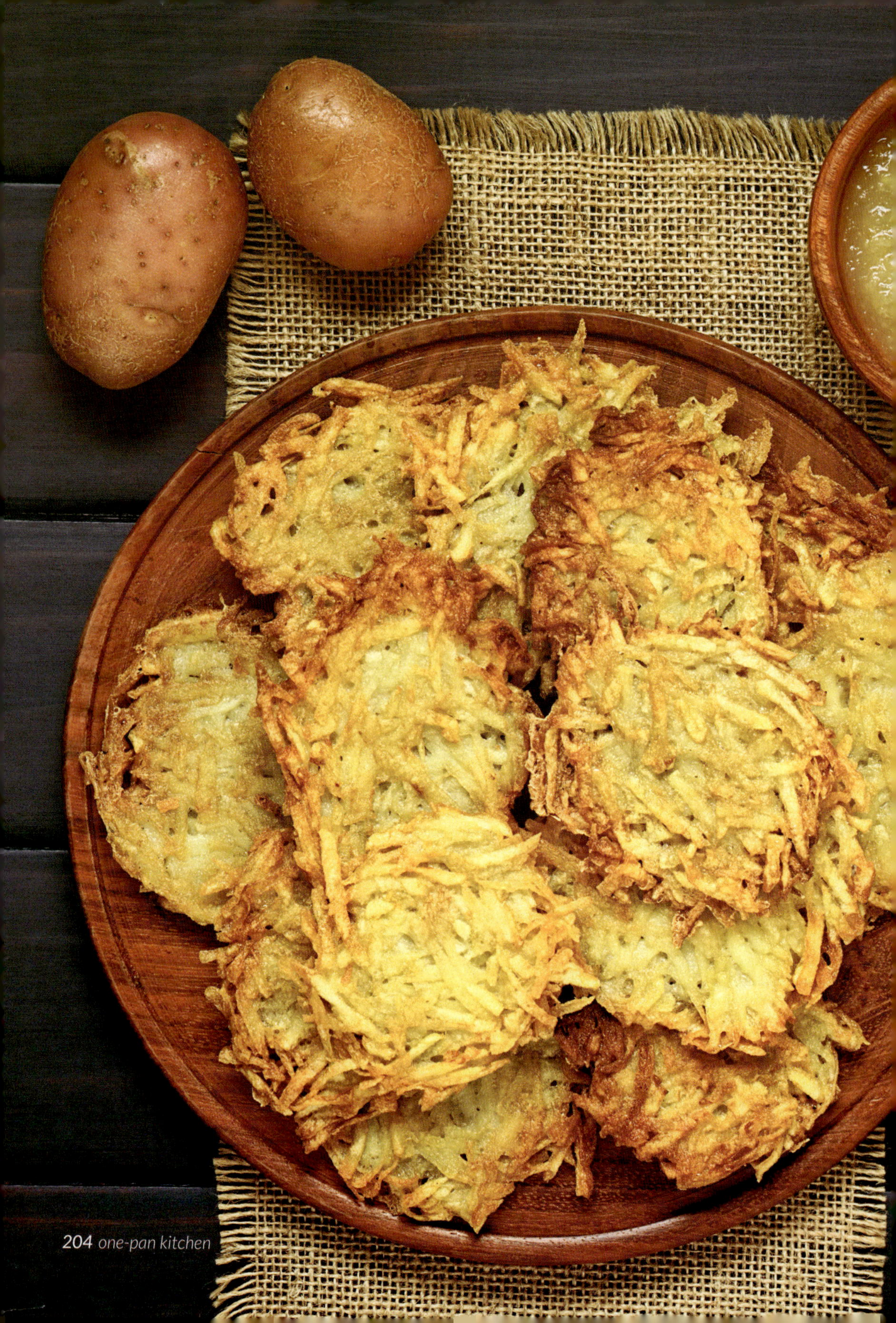

Potato Pancakes

Servings: 8 **Time:** 25 minutes

Ingredients

4 medium potatoes, peeled and shredded

2 eggs

1 yellow onion, diced

¼ cup flour

1 tsp onion powder

1 tsp salt

½ tsp pepper

¼ cup oil

Directions

In a large bowl, add all of the ingredients except for the oil and mix until well-combined.

Heat oil in the skillet on medium high heat. Scoop out potato mixture and form into small patties. Cook until potato pancakes are golden brown on both sides. Serve with Greek yogurt and apple sauce.

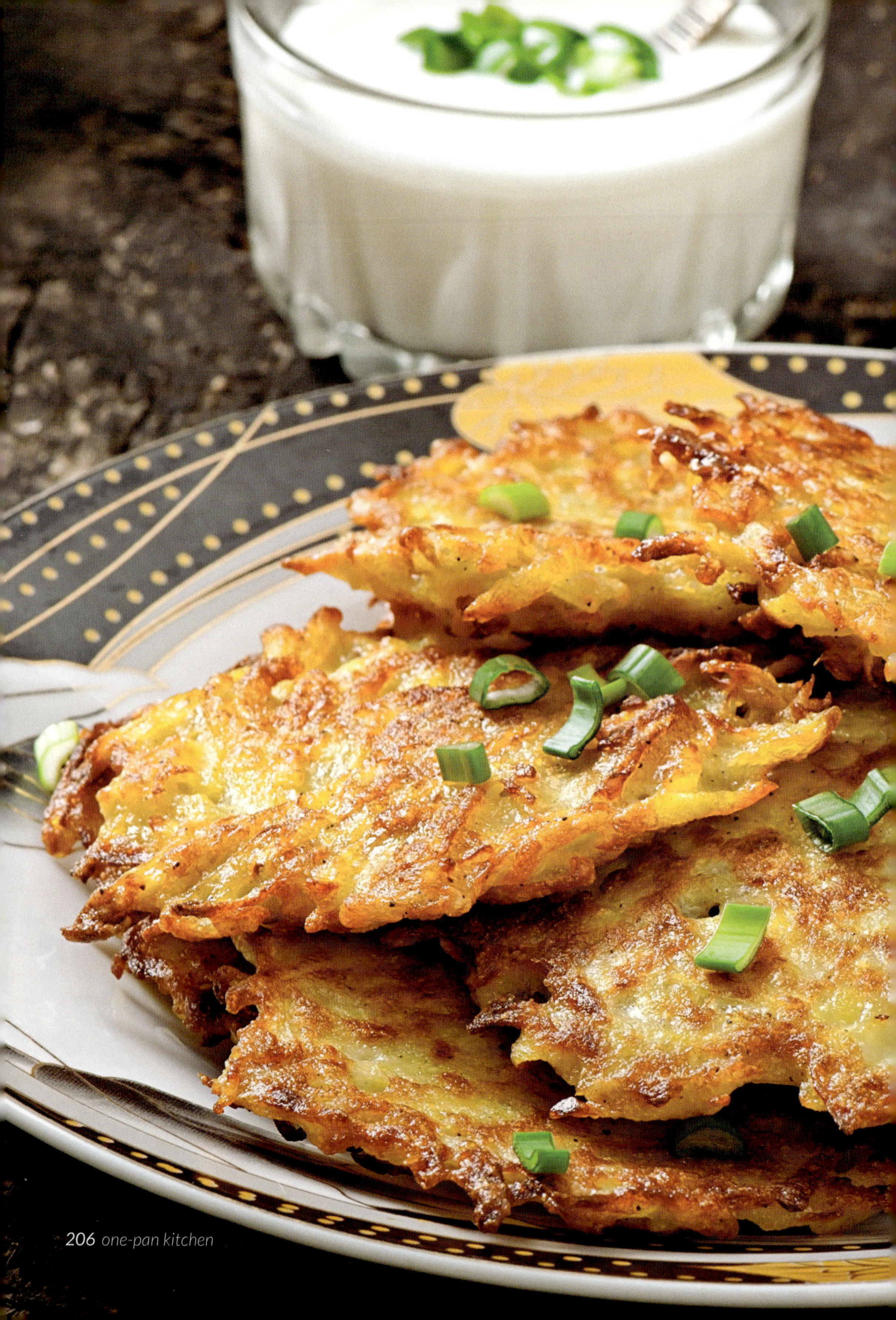

Sweet Potato Pancakes

Servings: 6 **Time:** 30 minutes

Ingredients

2 large sweet potatoes, peeled and shredded

2 eggs

1 yellow onion, diced

¼ cup flour

1 tsp kosher salt

¼ cup oil

Directions

In a large bowl, add all of the ingredients except for the oil and mix until well-combined.

Heat oil in the skillet on medium high heat. Scoop out sweet potato mixture and form into small patties. Cook until sweet potato pancakes are golden brown on both sides. Serve with Greek yogurt and apple sauce.

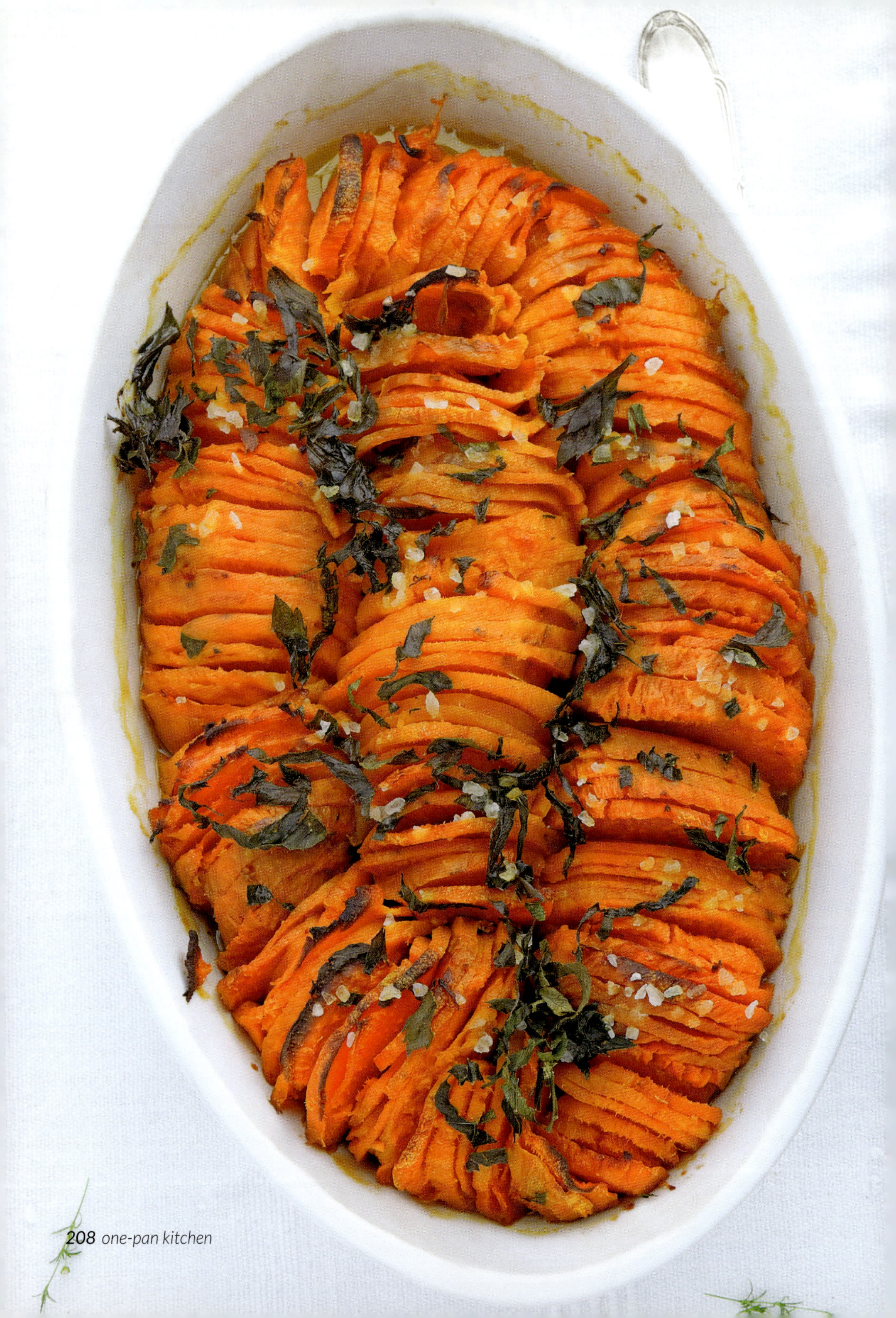

Roasted Yams with Orange Glaze

Servings: 6-8   **Time:** 45 minutes

Ingredients

4 yams, peeled and sliced thinly

3 tbsp butter

3 tbsp flour

2½ cups orange juice

salt and pepper, to taste

Directions

Melt butter in the skillet over medium heat. Whisk in flour and stir until mixture begins to brown.

Add orange juice and simmer until sauce thickens. Pour sauce into a pitcher. Layer sliced yams in the skillet, seasoning with salt and pepper between each layer.

Pour sauce over yams, cover, and cook on medium low heat for 30 minutes or until yams are soft.

210 *one-pan kitchen*

Sage Mashed Potatoes

Servings: 4-6   **Time:** 1 hour

Ingredients

½ cup (1 stick) butter

12 fresh sage leaves

6 large potatoes, peeled and quartered

1 cup Greek yogurt

salt and pepper, to taste

milk (optional)

Directions

Melt butter in the skillet on medium high heat. Add sage leaves and cook until crispy.

Remove sage from butter and reserve the butter. Wipe skillet clean. Add potatoes to the skillet and cover with water. Bring water to a boil on high heat and then lower to medium. Cook until tender.

Drain water. Mash potatoes with reserved butter, yogurt, milk (optional), salt, and pepper until creamy.

Garnish with sage leaves.

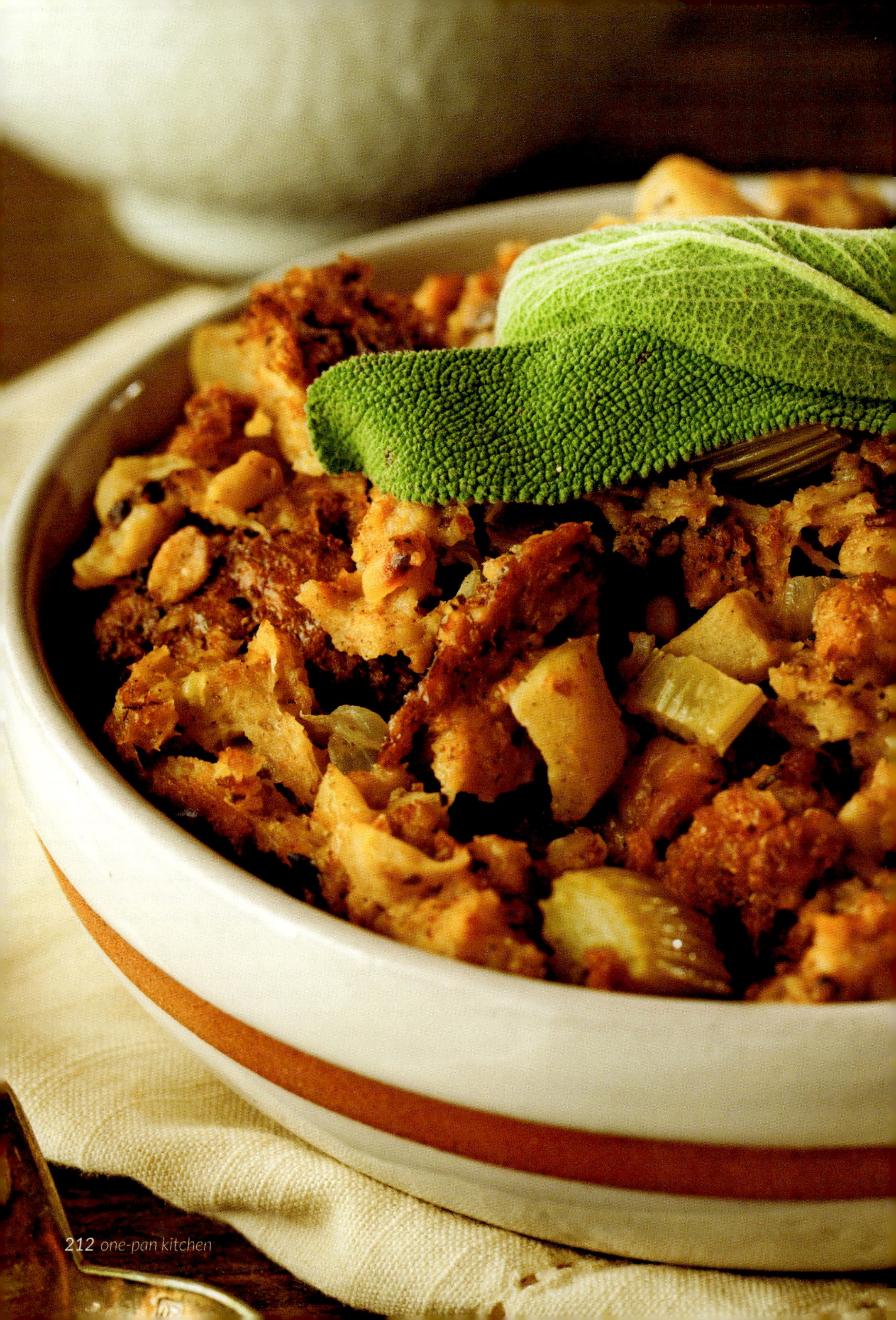

Sourdough Stuffing

Servings: 8-10   **Time:** 1 hour

Ingredients

2 loaves sourdough bread, cubed

2 onions, chopped

4 stocks celery, sliced

1 apple, cored and chopped

1 tbsp chicken base

1 tsp dried thyme

½ cup boiled cider

chicken or vegetable stock

salt and pepper, to taste

Directions

Melt butter in skillet over medium heat. Once melted, sauté onions, celery, and apples.

Cover skillet, turn to low, and let vegetables "sweat" until soft. Add chicken base, thyme, salt, pepper, and boiled cider to vegetables. Increase heat and bring to a boil.

Reduce the heat to low, cover, and simmer until the vegetables are very tender. Turn off the heat. Add bread cubes and stir, adding more boiled cider or some chicken (or vegetable) stock until bread is moistened.

Adjust seasonings. Turn heat to low. Cover and cook for 15 minutes or until the stuffing is heated through.

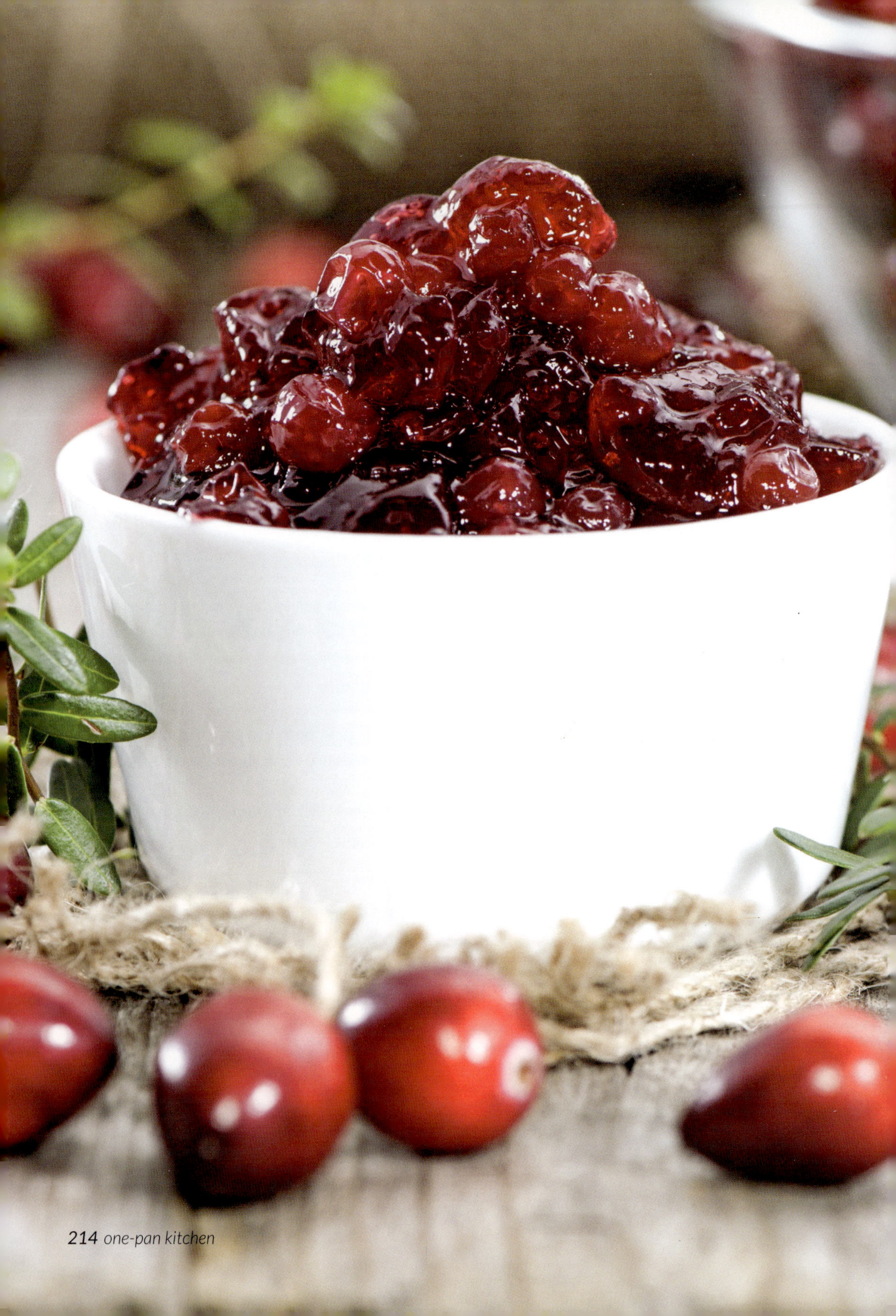

Spiced Cranberry Relish

Servings: 10   **Time:** 25 minutes

Ingredients

2 (12 oz) package cranberries

2 cups sugar

1½ cup water

6 whole allspice berries

6 whole cloves

2 cinnamon sticks

1 orange, zested

1 lime, juiced

Directions

Combine water, sugar, spices, and orange zest together in the skillet and bring to a boil. Decrease heat and simmer for ten minutes.

Remove spices from water and sugar mixture with a small mesh strainer. Add cranberries to skillet, increase heat, and bring to a boil. Cover skillet and turn off the heat. Let sit for 10 minutes.

The cranberries will soften and pop in the hot syrup. Add fresh lime juice. Refrigerate in jars until ready to serve.

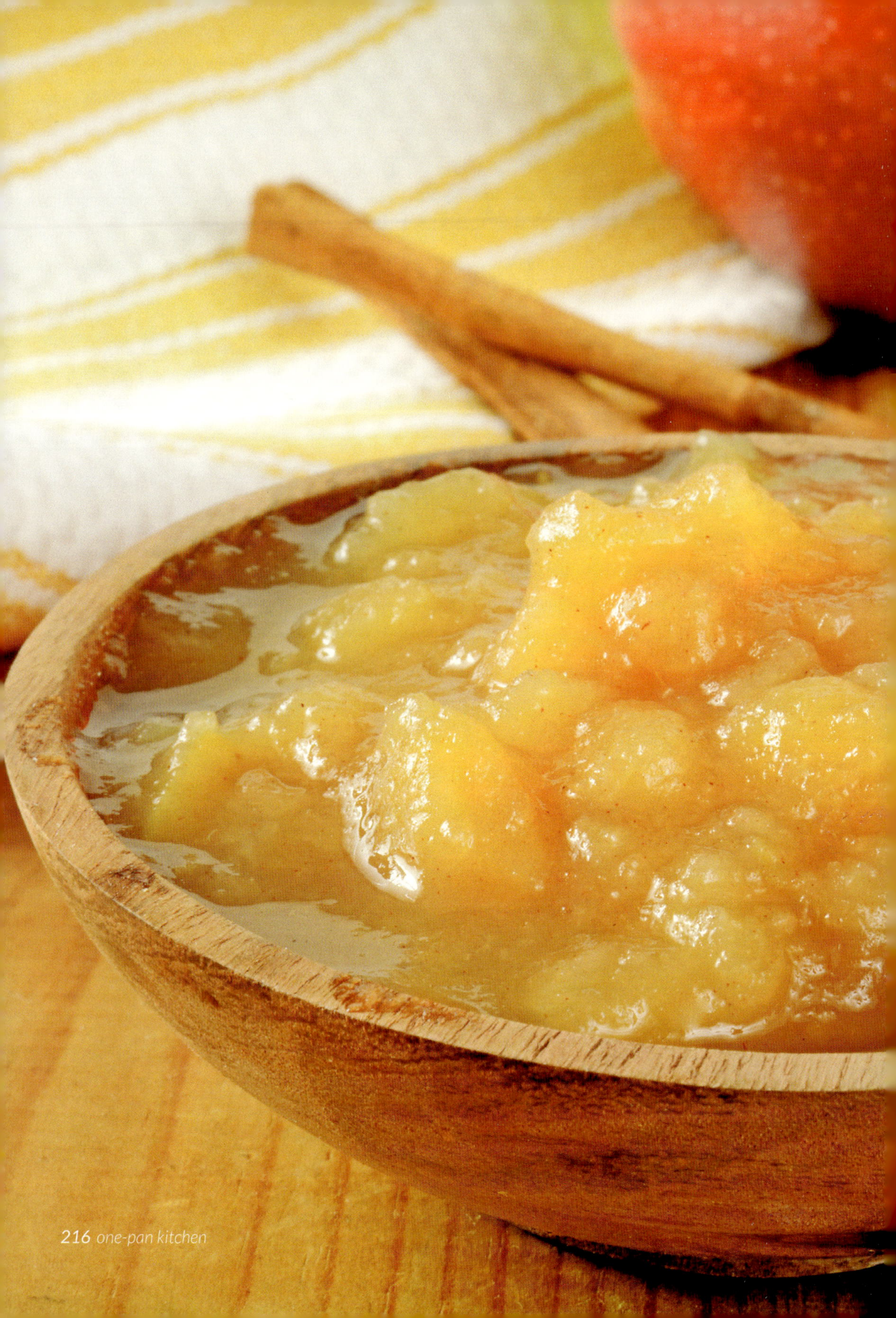

Cinnamon Apple Sauce

Servings: 10-12   **Time:** 30 minutes

Ingredients

12 apples, peeled and sliced

2 cups water

2 cinnamon sticks

Directions

Place all ingredients in the skillet and simmer on medium low heat with the lid on for 20 minutes or until the apples are soft.

Take out the cinnamon sticks and transfer the apples to a bowl. Mash to your desired consistency. Serve warm or chilled.

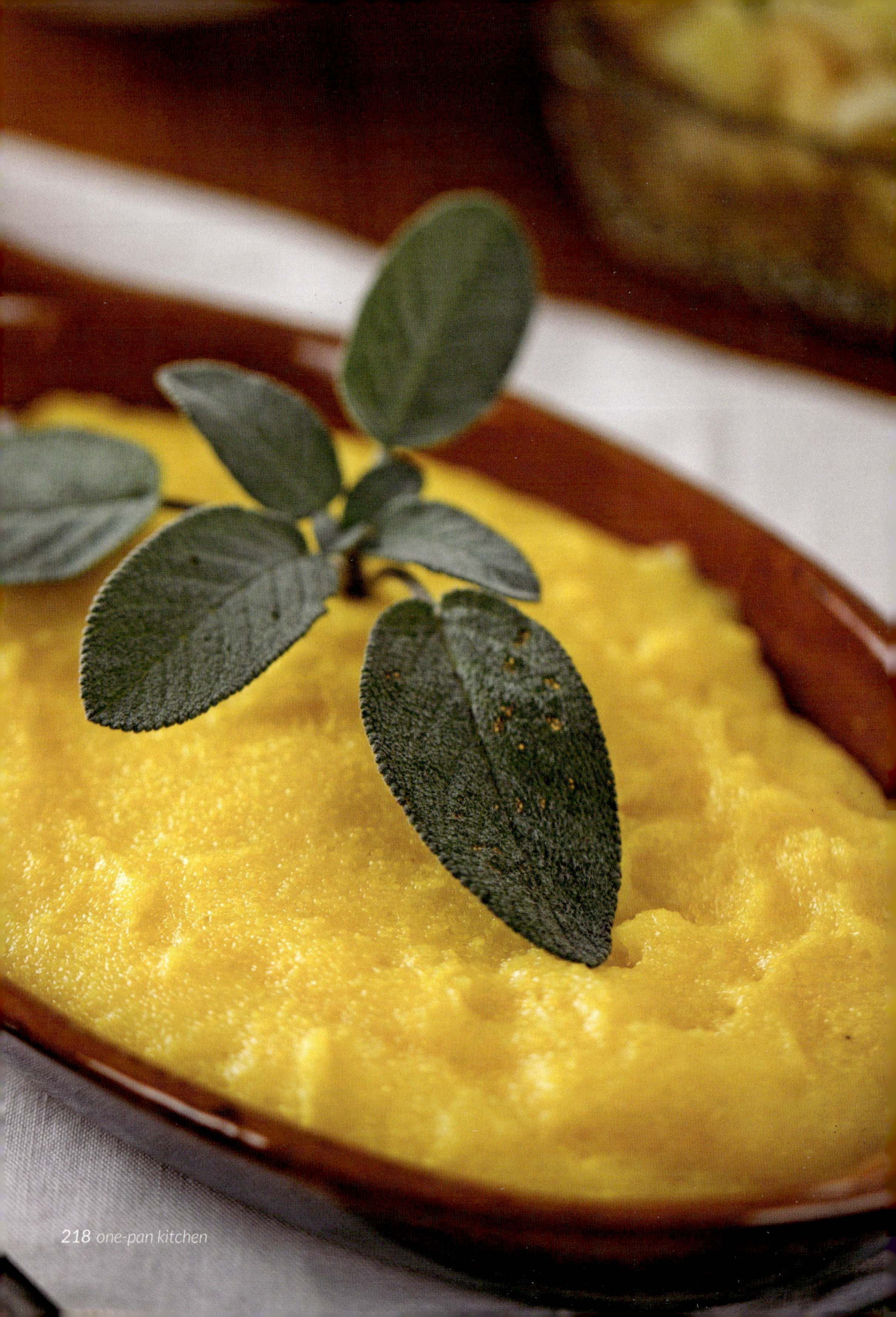

Skillet Polenta

Servings: 10-12   **Time:** 40 minutes

Ingredients

8 cups water

2 tsp salt

2 cups yellow cornmeal

1 cup Parmesan cheese

¼ cup (½ stick) butter

Directions

Boil water and salt in the skillet. Slowly add the cornmeal to the boiling water while whisking mixture. Stir mixture until it has thickened.

Cover the skillet and allow the polenta to cook on low for 30 minutes, stirring every 5 minutes so that the bottom does not burn.

Turn off the heat. Stir in the Parmesan cheese and butter before serving.

220 one-pan kitchen

Squash Risotto

Servings: 6   **Time:** 1 hour

Ingredients

½ butternut squash, peeled, seeded, and diced

4 tbsp butter

1 tsp salt

1 tsp smoked paprika

½ tsp crushed red pepper flakes

1 onion, chopped

1½ cup Arborio rice

7 cups chicken broth

½ cup Parmesan cheese

sage, to garnish

Directions

In the skillet on medium heat, melt 2 tablespoons of butter and sauté the squash with salt, red pepper, and smoked paprika until squash is tender.

Remove the squash from the skillet and add the remaining butter. Add the onion and Arborio rice. Turn the heat to low and mix in the broth, one cup at a time, while stirring gently. Wait for the broth to be absorbed by the rice before adding the next cup. Once the rice is tender, add ¾ of the cooked squash and the Parmesan cheese.

Season with salt and pepper to taste. Garnish with sage and the remaining squash.

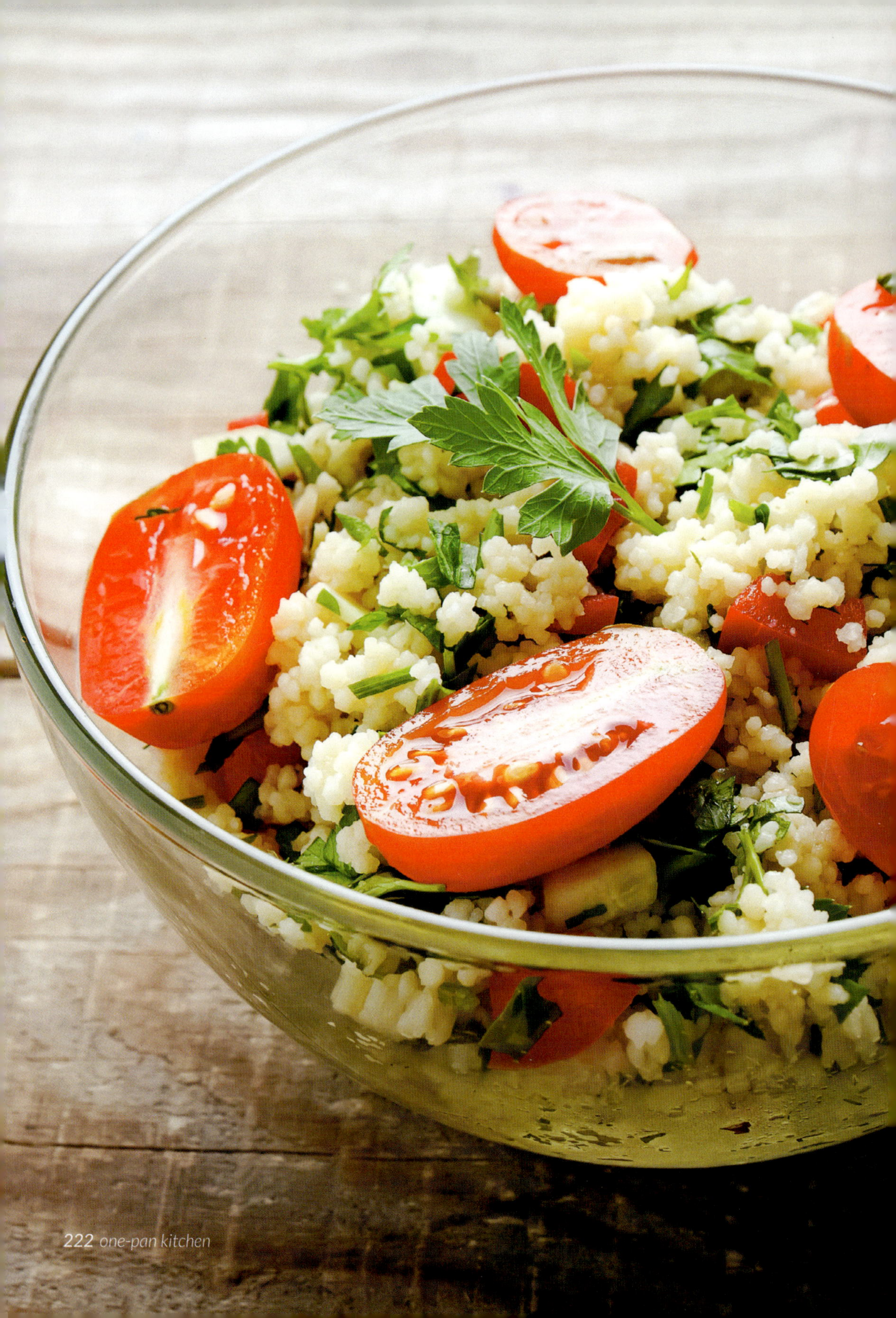

Couscous Salad

Servings: 8-10 **Time:** 15 minutes

Ingredients

4 cups water

3 cups plain, uncooked couscous

1 cup grated Parmesan cheese

6 tbsp fresh lime juice

½ cup olive oil

1 tsp salt

½ tsp freshly ground pepper

½ cup cilantro, minced

1 cup grape tomatoes, sliced

Directions

Boil the water in the skillet over high heat. Stir in the couscous and turn off the heat.

Cover the couscous and let sit for 5 minutes. Add the remaining ingredients and mix until well-combined.

Serve warm or chilled.

Steak and Strawberry Salad

Servings: 4-6   **Time:** 40 minutes

Ingredients

1 lb flank steak

1 tbsp olive oil

1 onion, thinly sliced

1 cup fresh strawberries, hulled and sliced

2 tbsp strawberry or raspberry jam

2-3 tbsp balsamic vinegar

1 cup sour cream

mixed salad greens

salt, to taste

freshly ground pepper, to taste

Directions

Coat the bottom of the skillet with olive oil. Heat the skillet over medium high heat until the oil is shimmering.

Add the onion slices and stir to coat. Spread the onions out evenly over the pan and lower heat to medium. Let cook, stirring occasionally to prevent the onions from burning or drying out. After 10 minutes, remove onions from heat and set aside.

Lightly grease skillet. Add steak and pan fry until cooked to your liking. Season with salt and pepper. Remove from skillet and let rest.

Add balsamic vinegar and jam to the skillet and bring to a light simmer. Turn off the heat and stir in the sour cream.

Add greens and onions to a salad bowl. Slice the steak into bite-size pieces and add to the greens. Top with fresh strawberries.

Pour the sour cream dressing over the salad. Toss to coat and serve.

Sweet Skillet Cornbread

Servings: 12 **Time:** 45 minutes

Ingredients

2 cups cornmeal

2 cups flour

1 1/3 cups sugar

1 tsp baking soda

1 tsp salt

4 eggs

½ cup oil

2 cups buttermilk

Directions

Sift together the dry ingredients. In a separate bowl, combine the wet ingredients and whisk. Make a well in the dry ingredients and pour in the wet ingredients. Mix until well-combined.

Lightly grease the skillet with a little olive oil. Then, pour the mixture into the pan.

Cook over medium heat with the lid on for 25 minutes or until puffy and golden on the edges.

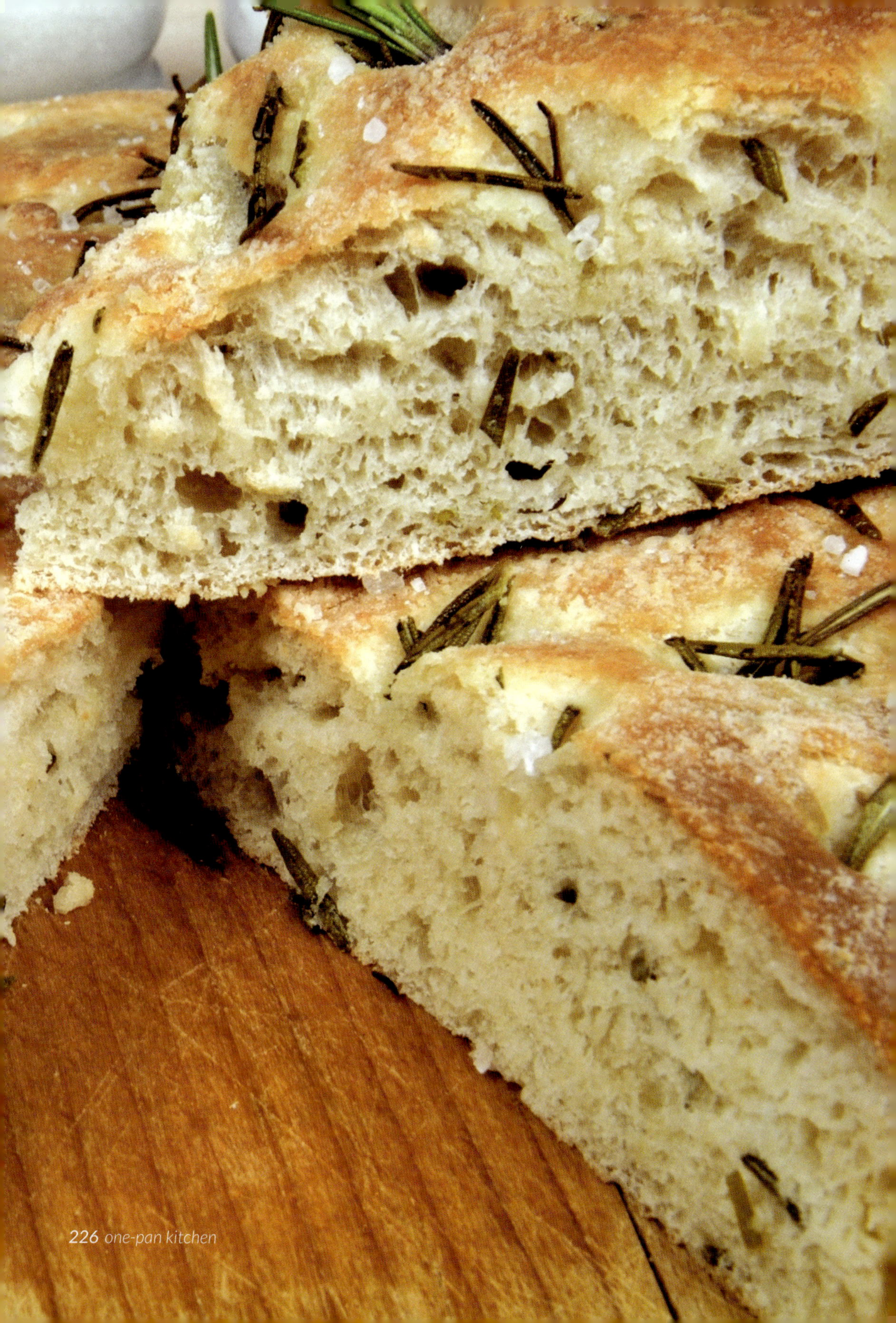

Focaccia Bread

Servings: 6-8   **Time:** 45 minutes

Ingredients

Dough:

1½ cups unbleached flour

1 tsp yeast

1 tsp salt

1 tbsp olive oil

¾ cup cold water

Toppings:

2 tbsp olive oil

½ tbsp coarse salt

freshly ground black pepper, to taste

1 tbsp fresh rosemary

Directions

Mix half of the flour, yeast, and salt in the bowl of a stand mixer with the paddle attachment.

Add cold water and olive oil while the machine is on low and mix for 1 minute. Add the rest of the flour and mix together. Increase the speed of the machine to high and continue to mix for 4-6 minutes.

Cover and leave on counter for at least an hour. Lightly grease skillet. Punch down the dough and roll out to fit your skillet. Poke holes in the top with a fork. Let dough rest for 15 minutes.

Brush the surface of the dough with olive oil. Place dough in the skillet with the oiled side down and bake, uncovered, for 5 minutes or until the bottom is crisp. Brush top of dough with olive oil and then flip. Top with salt, black pepper, and rosemary.

Cover and cook the focaccia on medium low for 15 minutes or until it is cooked through.

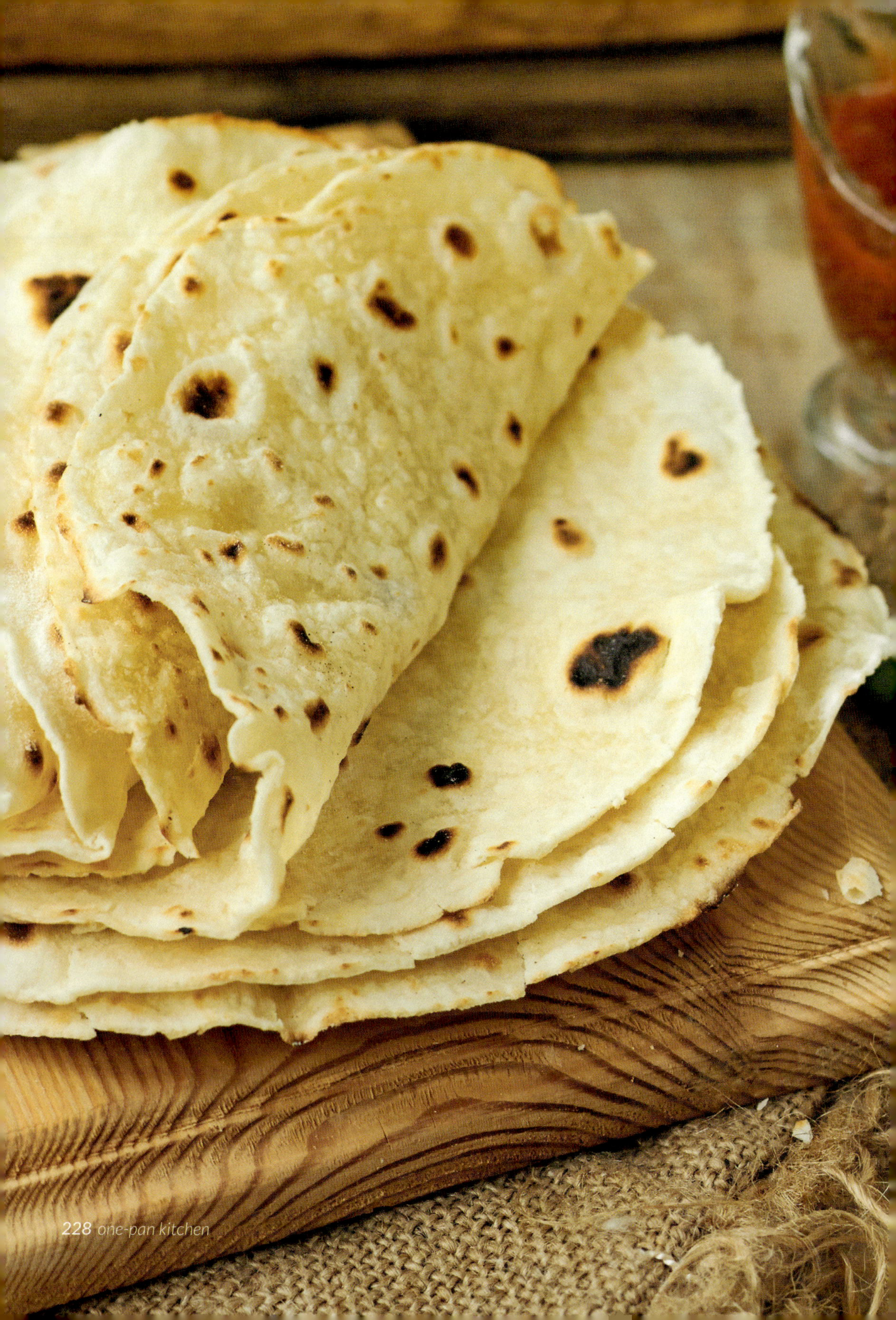

Homemade Tortillas

Servings: 8   **Time:** 25 minutes

Ingredients

2 cups all-purpose flour

½ tsp salt

3 tbsp olive oil

¾ cup water

1 tbsp butter

Directions

In a medium bowl, combine the flour and salt. Mix in the water and olive oil. Knead for 3 minutes or until the dough is smooth. Let dough rest for 10 minutes.

Cut dough into 8 chunks and roll out each chunk on a floured surface to an 8 inch diameter.

Melt butter in the skillet over medium high heat and cook tortillas for about 1 minute per side or until puffy and lightly brown.

Pineapple Upside Down Cake   pg 236-237

Desserts

232-233 Caramel Flan

234-235 Cranberry Pop Cake

236-237 Pineapple Upside Down Cake

238-239 Stone Fruit Crumble

240-241 Chocolate Peanut Butter Rice Puff Treats

242-243 Rice Pudding

244-245 Chocolate Pudding

246-247 Steamed Chocolate Pudding

248-249 Candied Nuts

250-251 Peach Jam

252-253 Butter Sauce

254-255 Butterscotch Sauce

256-257 Strawberry Soda Syrup

232 one-pan kitchen

Caramel Flan

Servings: 6   **Time:** 1 hour

Ingredients

1 cup white sugar

1 cup sweetened condensed milk

1 cup evaporated milk

1 tsp vanilla

6 egg yolks

Directions

In skillet, melt sugar on warm heat until it turns golden brown (watch carefully, it burns quickly). While sugar is melting, whisk together milks, vanilla, and egg yolks. Once sugar is golden, add about 2 tablespoons of the melted sugar to the bottom of 6 small, heatproof ramekins. Evenly divide filling between ramekins.

Wipe skillet clean. Add 2 cups water and place a stainless steel cooking rack into the skillet. Be careful not to scratch the cooking surface when inserting rack. Place filled ramekins on rack, cover with lid, and cook on medium heat for about 20-25 minutes until set. To serve, let flan cool to the touch, then run a butter knife around edges to loosen and invert over a plate.

Variations -

Chocolate: Reduce evaporated milk to ¾ cup, and add ¼ cup chocolate syrup.

Lemon: Replace vanilla with 2 tablespoons lemon zest.

Coconut: Replace evaporated milk with coconut milk.

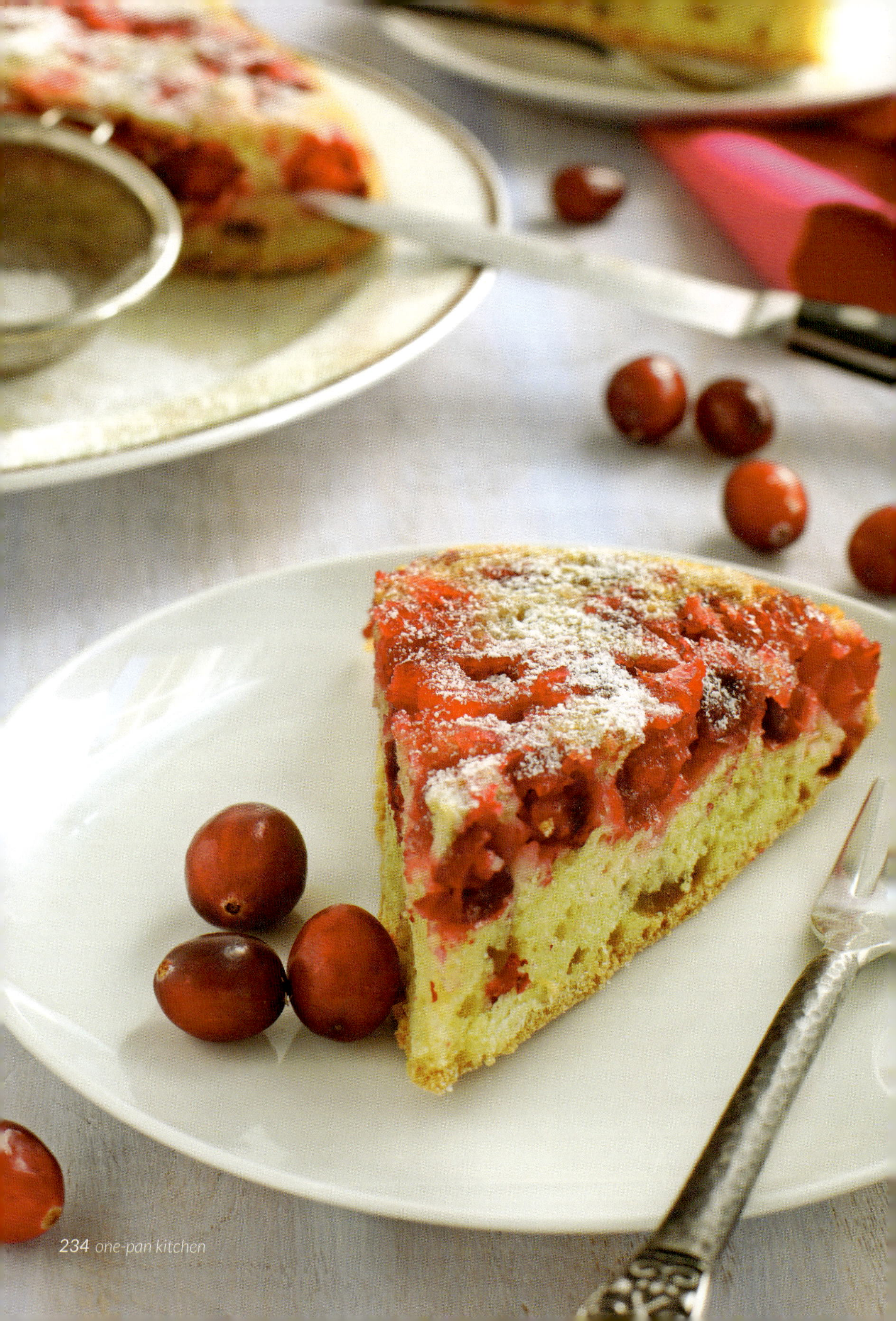

Cranberry Pop Cake

Servings: 8-10   **Time:** 30 minutes

Ingredients

6 tbsp butter

2 cups sugar

2 cups buttermilk

4 cups flour

2 tbsp baking powder

1 tsp salt

4 cups whole, fresh cranberries

Directions

Cream together butter and sugar. Add salt and baking powder.

Add flour alternately with buttermilk. Fold in cranberries.

Spoon into a greased skillet on medium low heat. Cover and bake for 25 minutes until a toothpick inserted comes out clean. Serve warm with butter sauce.

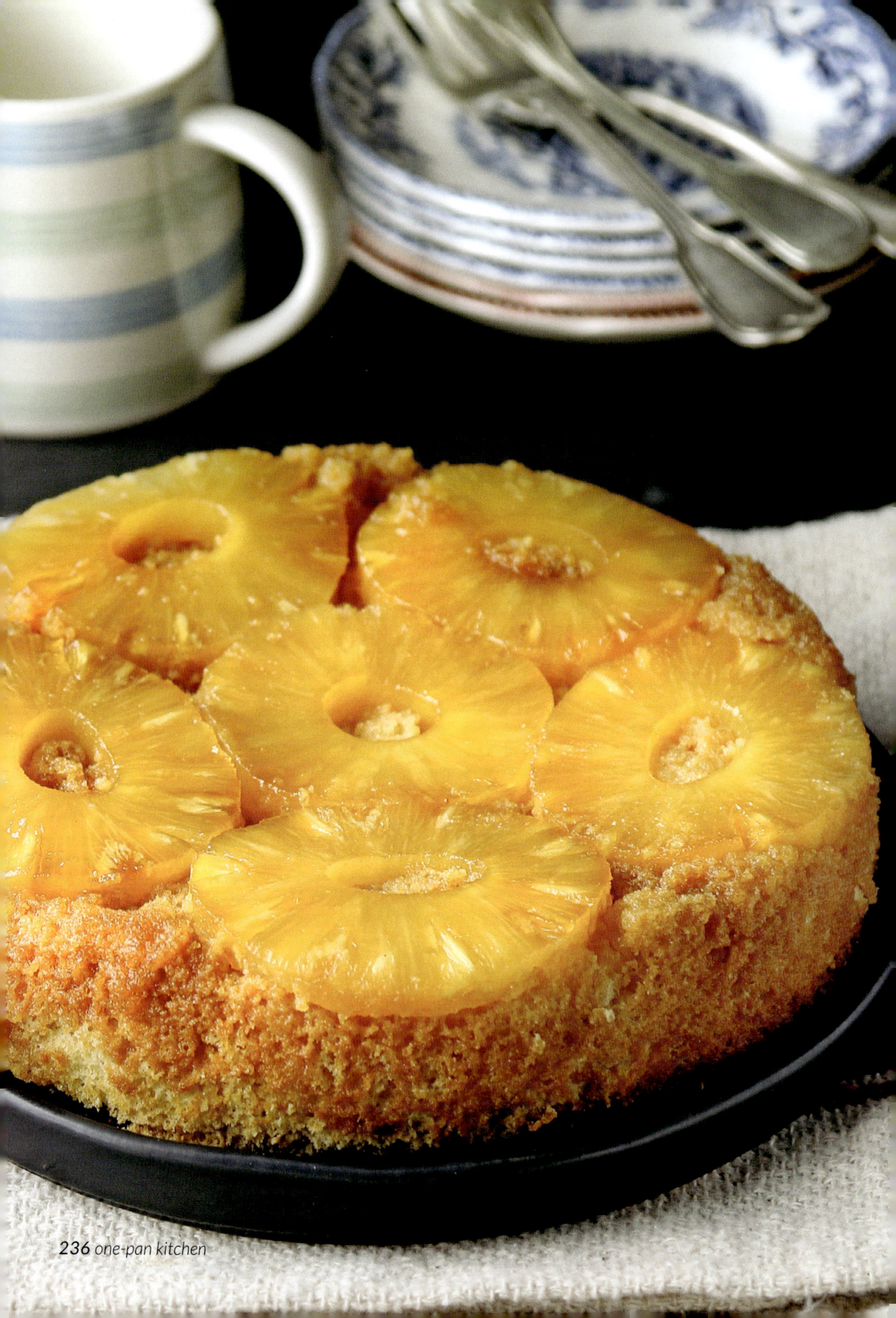

Pineapple Upside Down Cake

Servings: 24-36   **Time:** 1 hour

Ingredients

2 boxes yellow cake mix

eggs (see cake mix directions for amount)

oil (see cake mix directions for amount)

2 large cans sliced pineapple

1 stick butter

1 cup brown sugar

Directions

Drain pineapple and reserve juice. Prepare cake mixes according to package directions, using reserved pineapple juice in place of water.

Turn skillet to low, melt butter and brown sugar together. Carefully place pineapple rings over entire bottom of skillet on top of melted butter and sugar.

Pour prepared cake mix evenly over pineapple, cover with lid, and turn heat down to warm. Cook for 35-45 minutes until top is dry. Let cool for 5-10 minutes.

Place a plate or platter over the skillet and flip the skillet upside down so that the cake releases onto the plate.

238 one-pan kitchen

Stone Fruit Crumble

Servings: 8   **Time:** 20 minutes

Ingredients

4 peaches, diced

4 nectarines, diced

½ cup oats

4 tbsp coconut oil

2 tsp vanilla extract

2 tsp cinnamon

2 tsp salt

1 cup honey

2 cups walnuts

Directions

Melt coconut oil over medium heat in skillet. Add vanilla, cinnamon, salt, and honey to skillet and stir while simmering.

Then, add cut peaches and nectarines. Cook for 5-8 minutes, stirring and flipping constantly.

Remove from heat and put into bowl. Top with oats and walnuts.

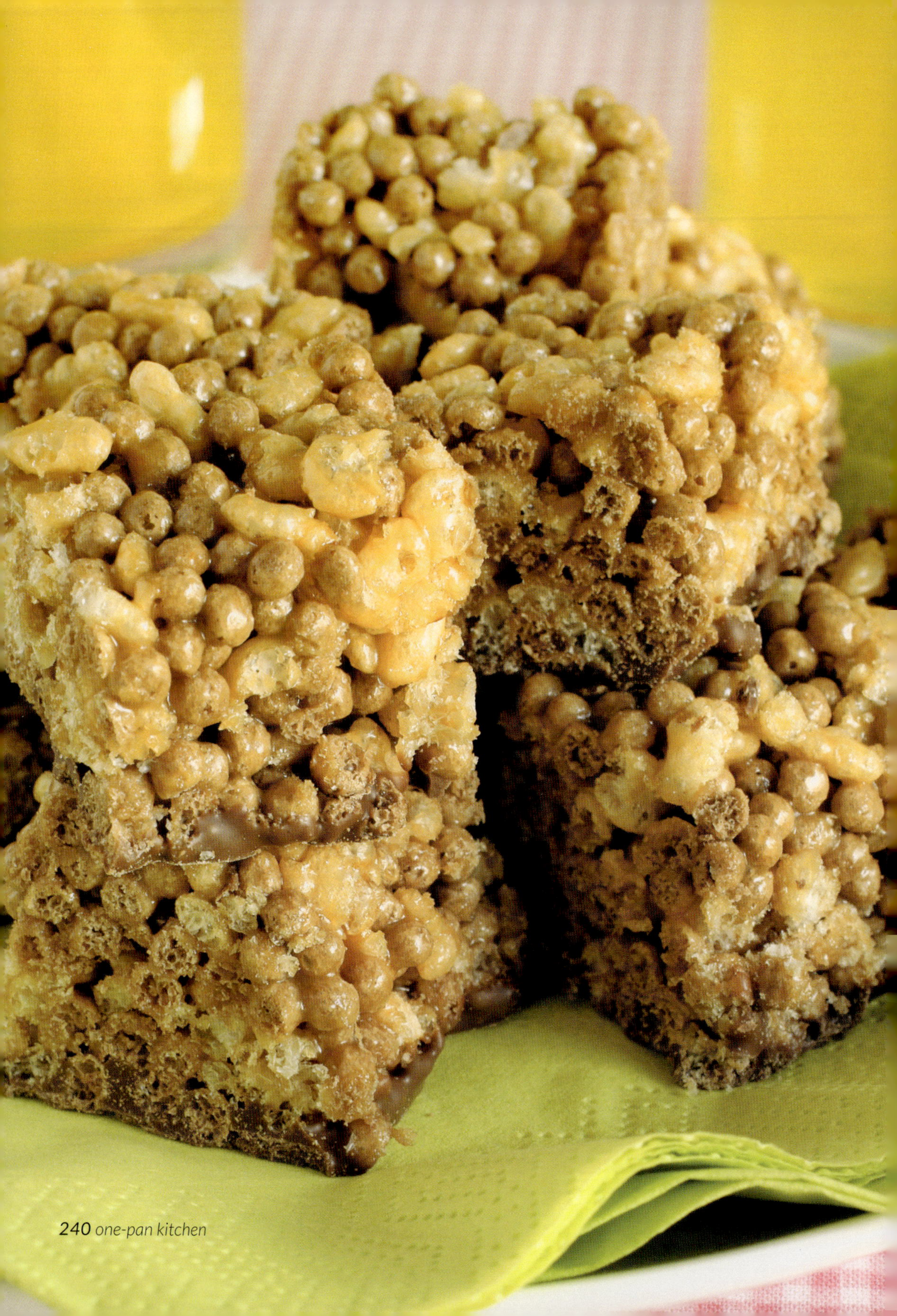

Chocolate Peanut Butter Rice Puff Treats

Servings: 48   **Time:** 30 minutes

Ingredients

3 cups peanut butter

3 tbsp vanilla extract

2 cups maple syrup

20 cups regular or brown rice puffs butter or vegetable oil, to grease

2 cups semi-sweet chocolate chips

Directions

In skillet, combine peanut butter, vanilla extract, and syrup. Bring to a simmer.

Turn off heat. Combine the rice puffs with the peanut butter mixture and stir until well combined.

Grease a baking dish with just enough oil so treats can be removed easily once cooled.

Press down rice puff mixture into a 9"x13" pan. Melt the chocolate chips in microwave (on low) and spread on top of rice puff mixture. Refrigerate for 30 minutes. Cut into squares and serve.

242 *one-pan kitchen*

Rice Pudding

Servings: 10 **Time:** 1 hour

Ingredients

4 large eggs

½ gal whole milk

1 cup rice

1 tsp salt

1 cup sugar

2 tsp vanilla or almond extract

cinnamon, for garnish

Directions

Combine milk, salt, and rice in the skillet on medium heat. Once mixture boils, reduce the heat to low, cover, and cook for 15 minutes. Remove lid and stir constantly for another 5-10 minutes or until the rice is tender.

Whisk sugar and eggs together and add mixture to the rice, stirring rapidly. Cook for 2 more minutes while stirring. Turn the skillet off and add almond or vanilla extract. Serve with cinnamon.

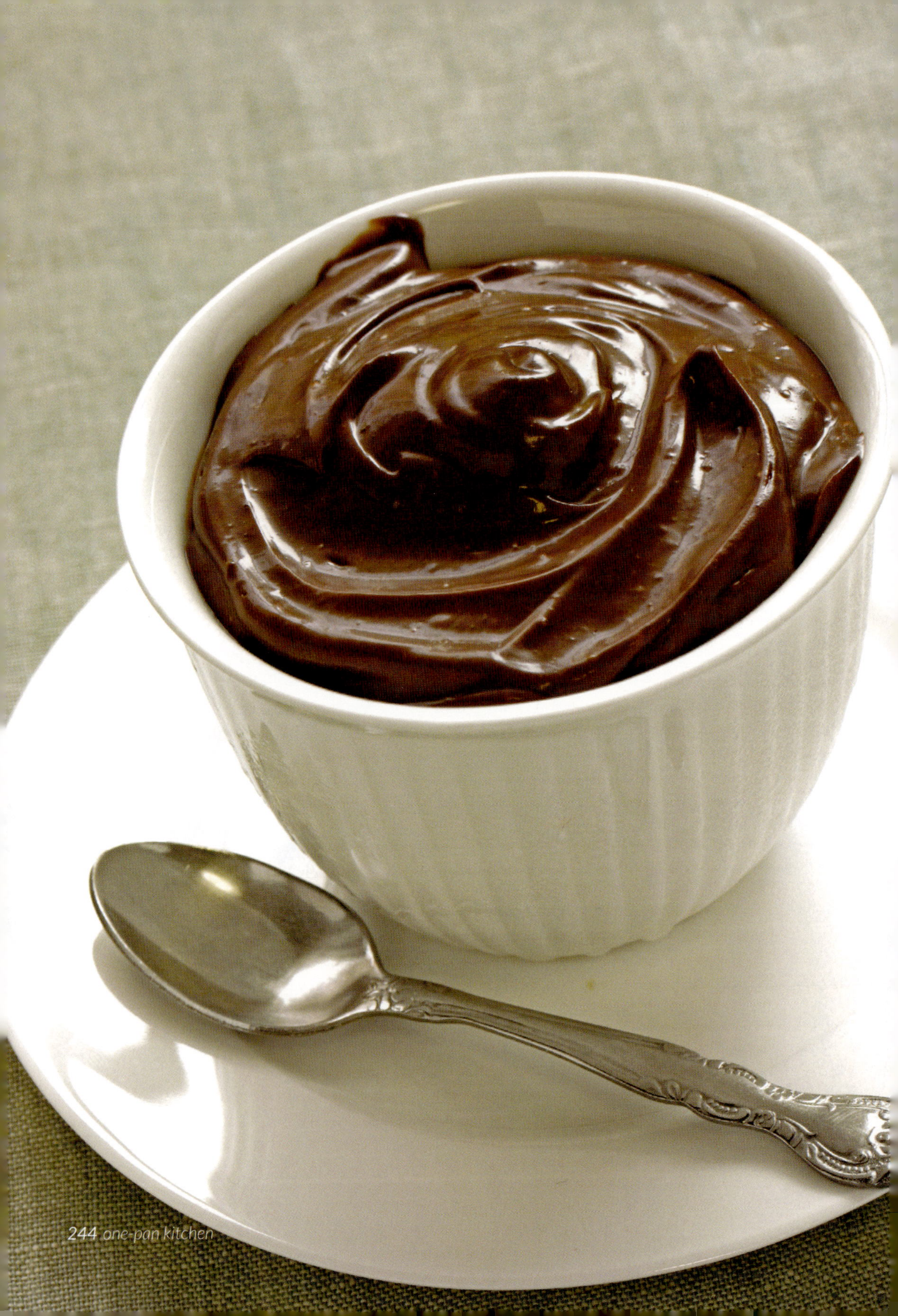

Chocolate Pudding

Servings: 16 **Time:** 15 minutes

Ingredients

1 cup sugar

½ cup cornstarch

¼ cup flour

1 cup unsweetened cocoa powder

pinch of salt

6 cups whole milk

2 cups heavy cream

24 oz semi sweet chocolate chips (about 4 cups)

2 tbsp vanilla extract

Directions

Whisk together sugar, cornstarch, flour, cocoa powder, and a pinch of salt in the skillet over low heat. Gradually stir in milk and cream.

Bring to a boil over medium high heat, whisking regularly until mixture is boiling. Whisk an additional minute while mixture is boiling. Turn off skillet.

Add chocolate chips and vanilla and let sit for a minute to soften the chocolate. Stir gently until chocolate is just melted. Serve warm or cold with fresh whipped cream.

246 one-pan kitchen

Steamed Chocolate Pudding

Servings: 4   **Time:** 25 minutes

Ingredients

1 cup flour

⅔ cup sugar

½ cup unsweetened cocoa powder

2 tsp baking powder

⅔ cup vegetable oil

1¼ cup milk

½ cup dark chocolate chips

Directions

Mix together the dry ingredients and then add the wet ingredients. Mix until well combined.

Gently place a stainless steel baking rack in the skillet and fill the bottom of the skillet with water up to the rack.

Spoon batter into 4 small ramekins and place ramekins on rack. Cover skillet and set to medium heat. Cook for 20 minutes or until pudding is set.

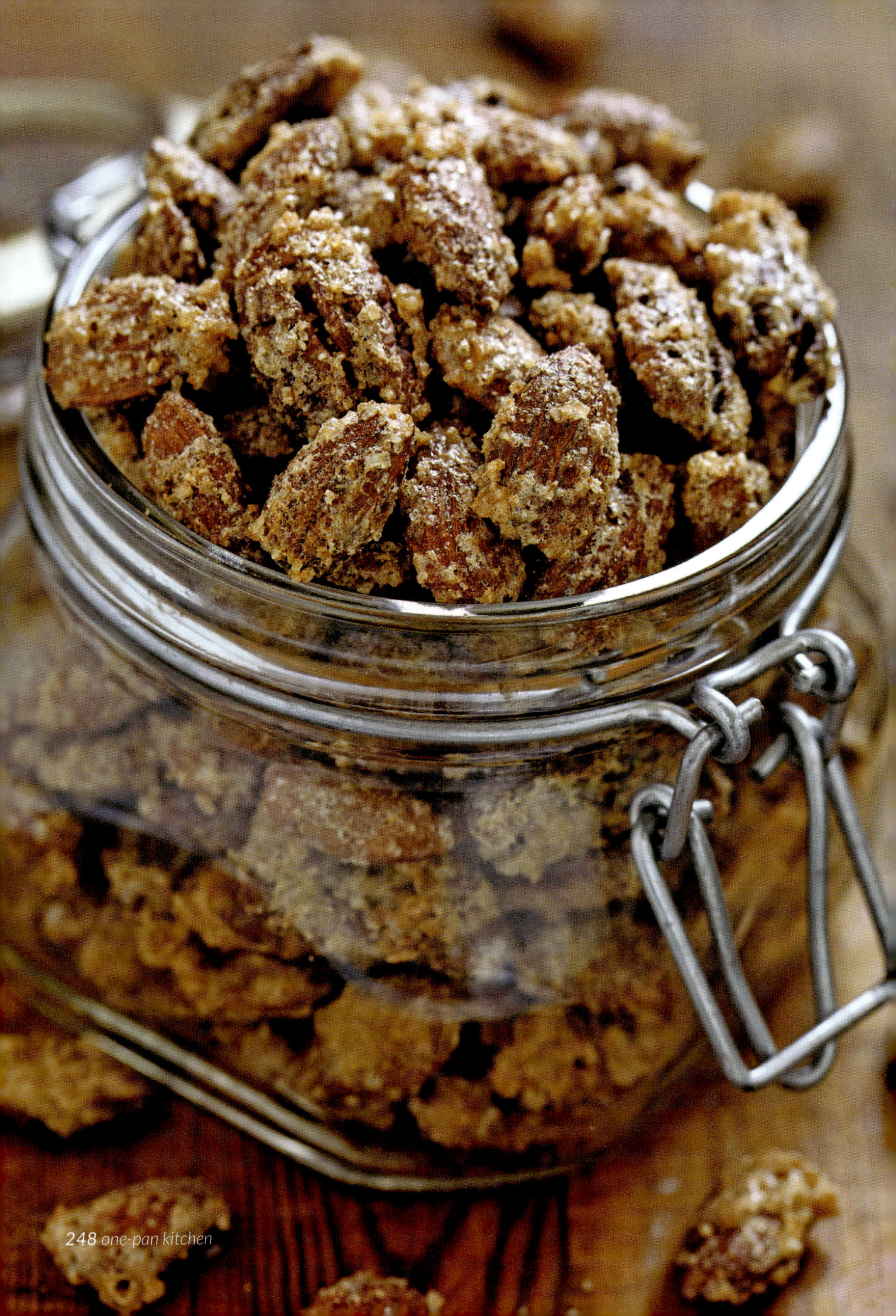

Candied Nuts

Servings: 8   **Time:** 15 minutes

Ingredients

1 cup raw pecans

1 cup raw almonds

2 tbsp coconut oil

¼ cup maple syrup pinch of sea salt

1 tsp ground cinnamon

Directions

Add pecans, almonds, and coconut oil to skillet and toast for 3 minutes over medium heat.

Once the nuts become fragrant, add the maple syrup, salt, and cinnamon.

Stir for a few more minutes until the maple syrup caramelizes. Then, remove from heat and spread on parchment to cool.

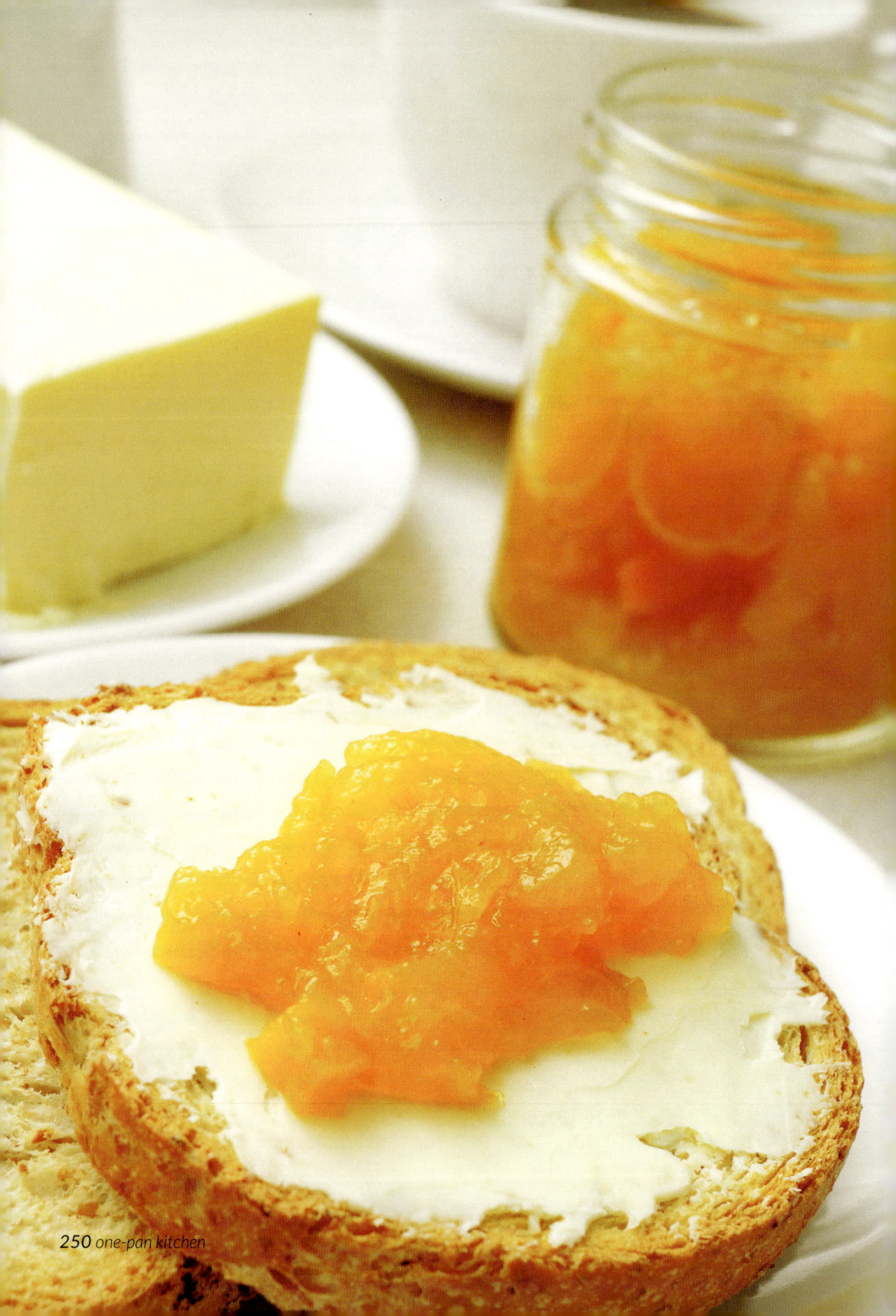

Peach Jam

Time: 1 hour

Ingredients

6 cups ripe peaches, peeled and sliced

½ cup honey

1½ lemons, juiced

Directions

Add peaches and lemon juice to skillet. Cook on medium high heat. Pour in honey and bring to a boil, stirring frequently, until honey dissolves.

Reduce to medium heat. Continue to cook the mixture until it thickens (about 25 minutes), stirring occasionally.

Turn off skillet and skim foam (if necessary).

Use a countertop or immersion blender to process the jam to the desired consistency.

Serve warm over french toast or allow to cool and store in refrigerator.

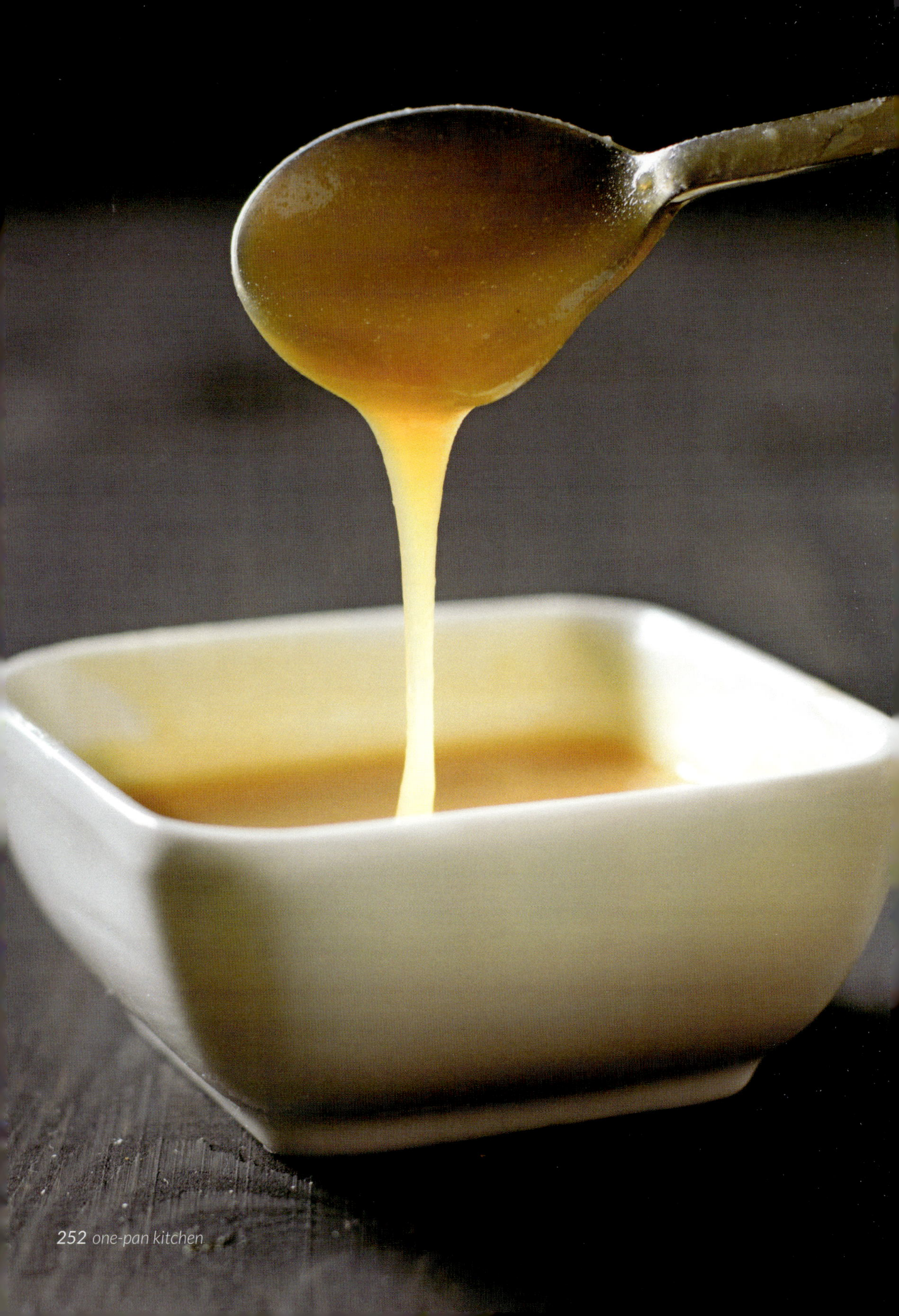

Butter Sauce

Servings: 12 **Time:** 10 minutes

Ingredients

½ cup butter
1 cup sugar
¾ cup cream
1 tsp vanilla

Directions

Combine butter, sugar, and cream in the skillet and bring to a boil. Reduce heat to low and simmer for 5 minutes.

Remove from heat and add vanilla.

Serve hot with warm cake.

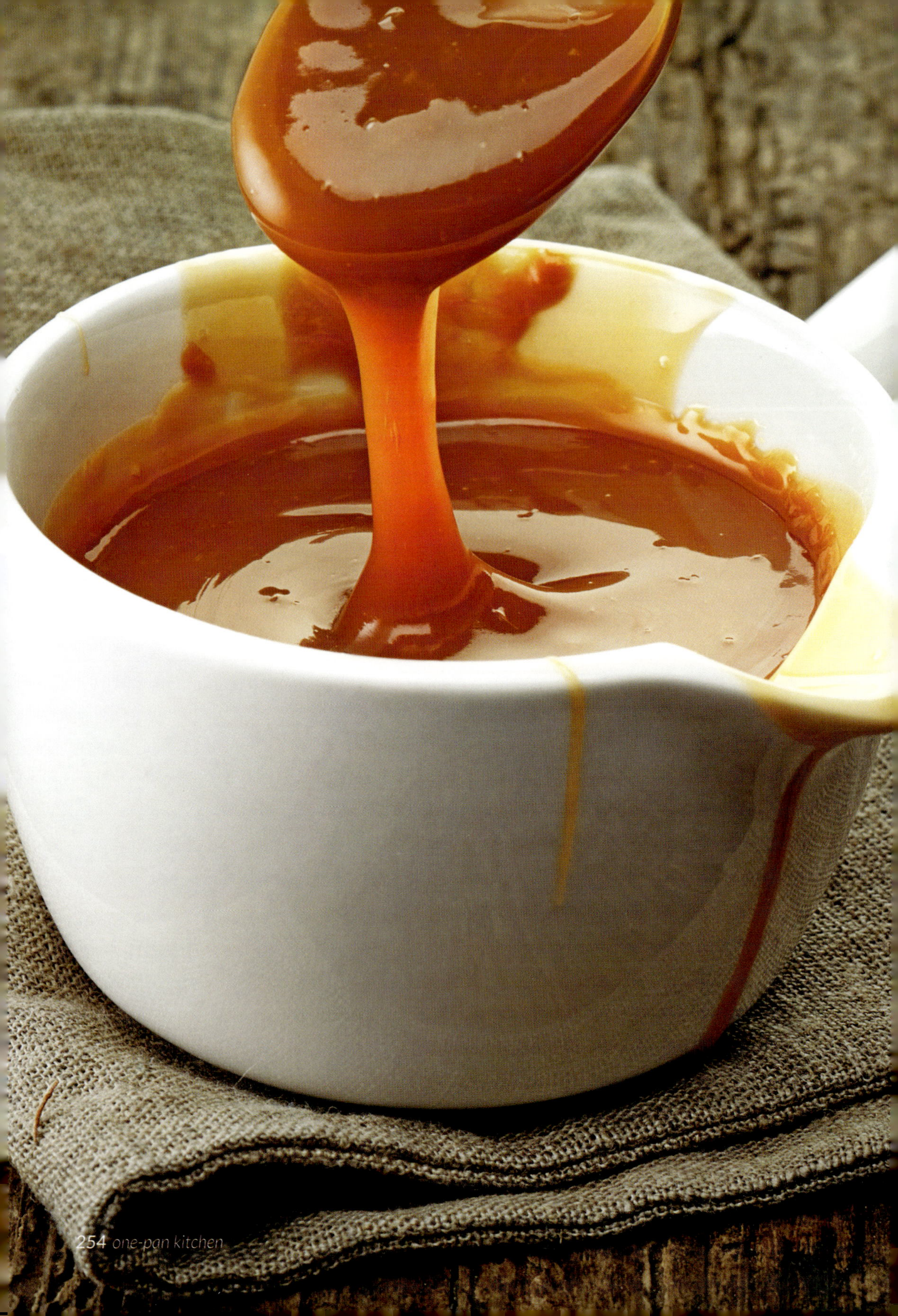

Butterscotch Sauce

Servings: 24-36   **Time:** 15 minutes

Ingredients

¾ cup butter

3 cups packed brown sugar

2 cups cream, divided

1½ tsp vanilla

1½ tsp salt

Directions

In the skillet over low heat, melt the butter with the sugar and ¾ cup cream, stirring until smooth.

Without stirring, let the mixture cook at a bubbling simmer for 3 minutes. Remove from the heat and stir in the remaining cream, vanilla, and salt.

The sauce is best served warm. It can be stored in a jar in the refrigerator for up to two weeks.

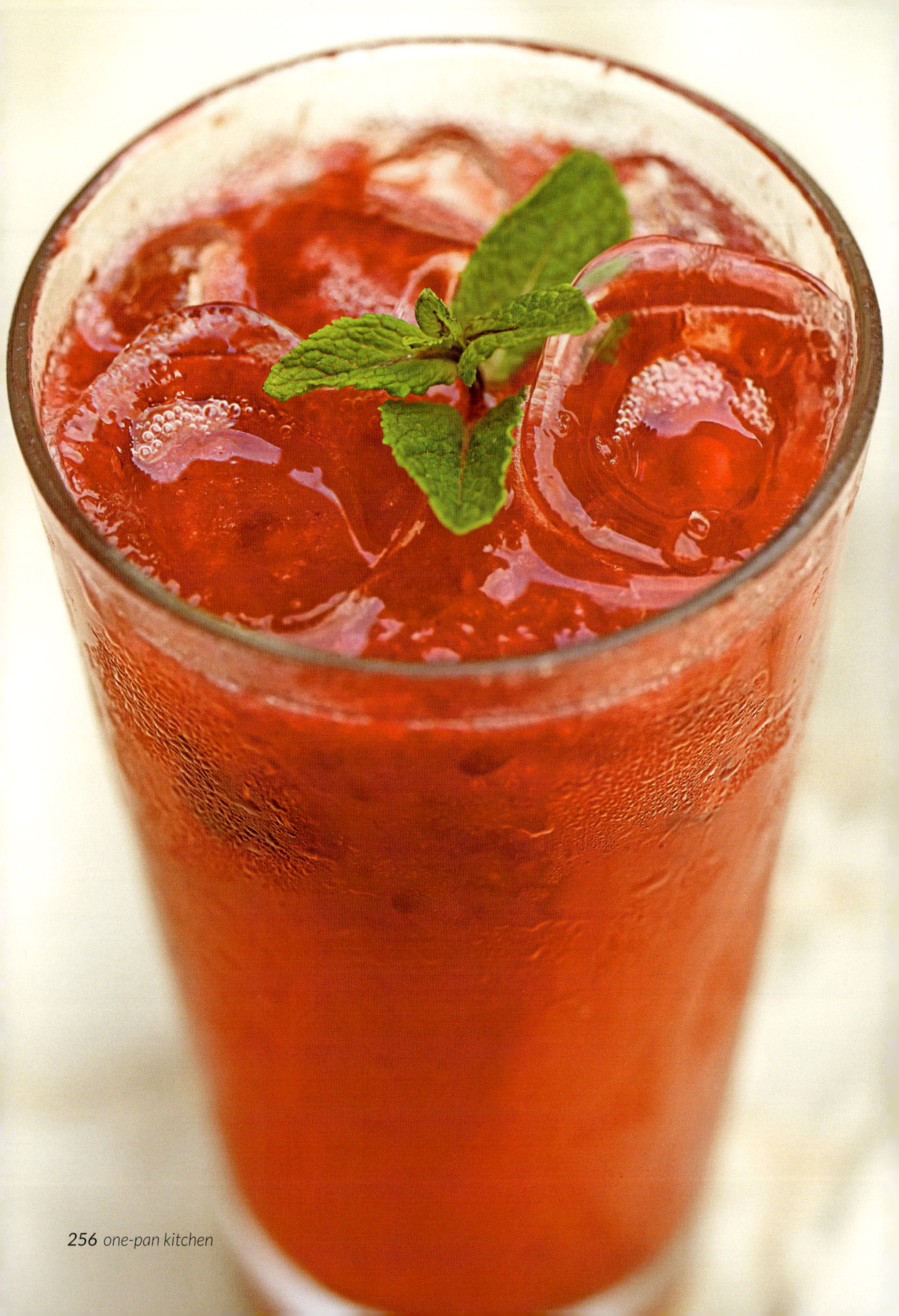

Strawberry Soda Syrup

Servings: 16   **Time:** 30 minutes

Ingredients

1 lb strawberries, stems removed and halved

1 lb rhubarb, chopped into ½" segments

1 cup sugar

1 cup water

1 lemon

sparkling water

Directions

Combine strawberries, rhubarb, sugar, and water in the skillet. Peel the lemon and add peel to the skillet.

Bring mixture to a boil and then reduce the heat to low. Simmer for 20 minutes or until fruit has completely collapsed, stirring occasionally.

Turn off heat, add the juice from the lemon, and let fruit cool in syrup for maximum infusion. Once cool, pour mixture through a strainer, pressing the solids with the back of a spoon or spatula to get the most syrup from them.

Pour into a glass bottle and chill until needed. To make 1 glass of soda, pour 2 tablespoons of the syrup in the bottom of a glass, fill with ice, and top with sparkling water.

Recipe Index

30 Minute Meals, 6-33

Macaroni & Cheese, Pg 8

Swiss Macaroni & Cheese with Mushrooms, Pg 10

Vegetable Stir-Fry, Pg 12

Moroccan Couscous, Pg 14

Skillet Pizza, Pg 16

Skillet Baked Ziti, Pg 18

Spicy Sausage Penne, Pg 20

Baked Tortellini, Pg 22

Chicken & Orzo Skillet Casserole, Pg 24

Chicken Schnitzel, Pg 26

Beef Quesadilla, Pg 28

Beef Fajitas, Pg 30

Meatballs & Mozzarella Bake, Pg 32

Breakfast, 34-51

Blueberry Yogurt Pancakes, Pg 36

Whole Wheat Pancakes, Pg 38

Cottage Cheese Pancakes, Pg 40

French Toast, Pg 42

Challah French Toast, Pg 44

Apple Cinnamon Breakfast Quinoa, Pg 46

Breakfast Hash, Pg 48

Tofu Scramble, Pg 50

Eggs, 52-69

Spanish Omelette, Pg 54

Steak and Egg Breakfast Wrap, Pg 56

Blissful Breakfast Scramble, Pg 58

Southwest Breakfast Scramble, Pg 59

Spinach Egg White Omelette, Pg 60

Cheese Strata, Pg 62

Basic Frittata, Pg 64

Butternut Squash & Sage Frittata, Pg 66

Tuscan Fritatta, Pg 68

Appetizers, 70-99

Game Day Nachos, Pg 72

Classic Buffalo Wings, Pg 74

Honey BBQ Wings, Pg 76

Sesame Ginger Wings, Pg 78

Yucca Fritters, Pg 80

Bacon Wrapped Dates, Pg 82

Spinach Pizza, Pg 84

Greek Pizza, Pg 86

Cranberry Meatballs, Pg 88

Tomato Spinach & Mozzarella Wrap, Pg 90

Chicken Quesadillas, Pg 92

Spinach and Artichoke Dip, Pg 94

Queso Dip, Pg 96

Garlic Crostini, Pg 98

Recipe Index

Soups & Stews, 100-127

Hearty Beef Stew, Pg 102

Classic Tomato Soup, Pg 104

Chickpea Stew, Pg 106

Garden Vegetable Soup, Pg 108

Lasagna Soup, Pg 110

Traditional Shepherd's Pie, Pg 112

Chicken Shepherd's Pie, Pg 114

Eggplant Curry, Pg 115

New England Clam Chowder, Pg 116

Cornbread Chili, Pg 118

Veggie Chili, Pg 120

Turkey and Black Bean Chili, Pg 122

Green Chili with Pork, Pg 124

White Chili, Pg 126

Entrées, 128-193

Mussels Mariniere, Pg 130

Paella, Pg 132

Ginger Garlic Shrimp Stir-Fry, Pg 134

Chipotle Shrimp Tacos, Pg 136

Lemon Pepper Cod, Pg 138

Pan Fried Tilapia, Pg 140

Crispy Skin Salmon, Pg 142

Buttermilk Fried Chicken, Pg 144

Thai Peanut Curry, Pg 146

Red Curry, Pg 148

Chicken Parmigiana, Pg 150

Chicken Pizzaiola, Pg 152

Lemon Chicken with Spinach and Mushrooms, Pg 154

Apricot Chicken with Bell Peppers, Pg 156

Rosemary Steak, Pg 158

Classic Cheese Burger, Pg 160

Mumma Bumma's Meatballs, Pg 162

Classic Tomato Sauce, Pg 164

Italian Style Meatballs, Pg 166

Classic Lasagna, Pg 168

Firehouse Chili, Pg 170

Korean Bbq Beef, Pg 172

Pepper Beef, Pg 174

Pear & Ginger Pork, Pg 176

Pork Chops with Apple Gravy, Pg 178

Hearty Cornbread Dressing, Pg 180

Carnitas Pizza, Pg 182

Eggplant Parmigiana, Pg 184

Korean Stir-Fried Noodles (Japchae), Pg 186

Zucchini Burger, Pg 188

Gourmet Grilled Cheese, Pg 190

Butternut Squash & Kale Linguine, Pg 192

Recipe Index

Sides, 194-229

Garlic Broccoli, Pg 196

Pan-Seared Brussel Sprouts, Pg 198

Pine Nut and Ginger Broccoli, pg 200

Sautéed Root Vegetables, Pg 202

Potato Pancakes, Pg 204

Sweet Potato Pancakes, Pg 206

Roasted Yams with Orange Glaze, Pg 208

Sage Mashed Potatoes, Pg 210

Sourdough Stuffing, Pg 212

Spiced Cranberry Relish, Pg 214

Cinnamon Apple Sauce, Pg 216

Skillet Polenta, Pg 218

Squash Risotto, Pg 220

Couscous Salad, Pg 222

Steak and Strawberry Salad, Pg 224

Sweet Skillet Cornbread, Pg 225

Focaccia Bread, Pg 226

Homemade Tortillas, Pg 228

Desserts, 230-257

Caramel Flan, Pg 232

Cranberry Pop Cake, Pg 234

Pineapple Upside Down Cake, pg 236

Stone Fruit Crumble, Pg 238

Chocolate Peanut Butter Rice

Puff Treats, Pg 240

Rice Pudding, Pg 242

Chocolate Pudding, Pg 244

Steamed Chocolate Pudding, Pg 246

Candied Nuts, Pg 248

Peach Jam, Pg 250

Butter Sauce, Pg 252

Butterscotch Sauce, Pg 254

Strawberry Soda Syrup, Pg 256